Also by the Author

Paul, Apostle of Weakness

Linguistics for Students of New Testament Greek

New Testament Criticism and Interpretation

Scribes and Scripture

Linguistics and New Testament Interpretation

Using New Testament Greek in Ministry

New Testament Textual Criticism

It's Still Greek to Me

The Myth of Adolescence

The Holy Bible: International Standard Version New Testament

Interpreting the New Testament

Rethinking the Synoptic Problem

Here I Stand

Why Four Gospels?

Rethinking New Testament Textual Criticism

The New Testament: Its Background and Message

Why I Stopped Listening to Rush

Perspectives on the Ending of Mark

Learn to Read New Testament Greek

What Others Are Saying

The Jesus Paradigm is a personal and passionate appeal for real discipleship, just the kind of plea that *Christians* need to hear. This is also a plea for the church to be what it was called to be, something far different from most of what we see. People may disagree with parts of the book, but they cannot legitimately ignore its challenge.

Klyne R. Snodgrass, Paul W. Brandel Professor of New Testament Studies, North Park Theological Seminary

This is an excellent book. Well written, accessible, challenging, reasonable for the most part. There is no higher compliment that I can give a book than to say it was challenging to me, made me want to read the Scriptures more diligently, and that I marked pages and quotes liberally. This book did all three.

Arthur Sido, Blogger at *The Voice of One Crying Out In Suburbia*

Here is a book that calls for nothing less than the complete dismantling of business-as-usual in the twenty-first century church in favor of a radical model based entirely on Scripture and rediscovered by the sixteenth century Anabaptists. Black writes an immensely practical book that will rearrange the furniture in your mind and, if heeded, will resurrect biblical Christianity.

David B. Capes, Professor in Christianity, Houston Baptist University

Black's purpose in writing this book is to encourage his readers toward "radical discipleship." He is concerned (rightfully so, I would say) that many believers have forfeited following Jesus, and have instead placed their trust in their traditions, their leaders, or their politics. This book is strictly about discipleship, about following Jesus in the simple – yet extraordinarily radical – ways in which Scripture describes and prescribes. This is a book I would recommend to anyone. Read it, share it with others, then live the pattern of life that you find in Scripture – the pattern of life in which only the Holy Spirit can direct you and empower you.

Alan Knox, Blogger at *The Assembling of the Church*

The church is set to undergo massive transformations in the coming years and decades. Many great authors have recently been describing desired and/or emerging models; David Alan Black is among them with his newest book, *The Jesus Paradigm*. Black offers more than the Anabaptist tradition as a model; he offers Jesus as a paradigm. The self-giving love and service that we find in our God who gave his only begotten Son is the foundation from which he seeks to work. Jesus' peace should look completely opposite from *Pax Romana* or *Pax Americana*. Jesus' ministry is about service, not power and prestige. The church in our age and all the ages has failed miserably at taking up our cross. As our contemporary church is focusing on self-help and "me-centered" gospels, Black offers the only faithful alternative – the cross of Christ.

Geoffrey Lentz, Associate Pastor, First United Methodist Church, Pensacola, Florida

This book could and should change your life. Put it at the top of your reading list. It will do one of three things: reinforce your beliefs, challenge your beliefs, or make you write it off as rubbish. But do read the book.

Jack Watkins, Blogger at *Flight Level Musings*

Some who read this book will think Dave Black has gone too far; some will think he has not gone far enough. But as he himself says about one of his own sources, "One does not have to agree with everything in the book to appreciate it." Few readers will appreciate all aspects of Black's argument, but it is high time we all heard and heeded its radical, sobering, and exciting call to the Church of Jesus Christ simply to obey her Master!

Richard J. Erickson, Associate Professor of New Testament, Fuller Theological Seminary

This book calls the reader back to a simple faith, a life of simple obedience to the calling of Christ. Dr. Black is a respected scholar, but the things he shares in this work did not come from time in the library, but rather from time spent with the neglected, poor, humble, and forgotten – the same types that Jesus spent His time with. I would encourage any follower of Jesus to read this book. It will challenge your thinking. May God use it to bring His church closer to Himself!

Jon Glass, Pastor, Cresset Baptist Church, Durham, North Carolina

Black's purpose in this book is to ask his readers to rethink what they see as Christianity today, and instead recognize it as a "Christendom" that Christ never called them to. According to Black, this "Christendom" is a politicized, self-serving thing Christ did not want, but instead stood against. He sees the state of discipleship in America being sadly neglected. Black wants all members of the Church involved in the Body of Christ. You may not agree with everything Black says, but it will force you to wrestle with issues that you might not think about otherwise.

Matt Evans, Blogger at *Broadcast Depth*

The Jesus Paradigm is revolutionary, but it is also simple. It is challenging, but it is also relatively easy to read. The reason for these things is that Dr. Black is simply trying to be as biblical as he can. I encourage every Christian to read this book. Even if you do not agree with all the author says, it will cause you to think.

Eric Carpenter, Pastor, Chevis Oaks Baptist Church, Savannah, Georgia

"Brother David" delivers a punch in the gut of cultural Christianity, whether on the right or the left. He pokes and prods the church to be a "radical, Christ-centered, martyr movement." This reincarnation of a sixteenth century Anabaptist is guaranteed to stir you up, regardless your church niche. If you are confused or irritated by the current culture wars, let this seasoned and salty Jesus follower draw you to the center he has found.

Kent L. Yinger, Associate Professor of New Testament, George Fox Evangelical Seminary

David Alan Black, in his just released book *The Jesus Paradigm*, presents the simplicity of the early church in worship and discipleship and points out how far we have drifted from this ideal model. His book may be controversial (radical by some standards) but his views are heartfelt. People will be blessed in reading his book even if some may feel their toes being stepped on.

Bob Makar, Author and Blogger at *The Messiah Road Map*

Many have deep questions about American Churchianity and even Evangelicalism, but are not sure if it's okay to ask. A respected scholar with a missionary heart, Dave invites you along his journey. What a few of my generation were whispering, a flood of younger American Christians are shouting. Weary of fighting with fellow believers over secondary or tertiary doctrine, they are seeking a community of radical disciples. Arguing Jesus gave us a paradigm (Jn. 13:15), Dave passionately suggests "The American church has forgotten this servant role of Christianity." Black offers us more than the pseudo-radicalism of many popular Christian speakers who condemn the materialism of the church while modeling a careerism as secular as their leadership principles. Dave calls us back to the Jesus paradigm.

E. Randolph Richards, Dean of the School of Ministry and Professor of Biblical Studies, Palm Beach Atlantic University

The Jesus Paradigm is not for the faint-hearted; in fact the road may be hard and lonely. But Brother Dave not only says what needs to be said, he is striving to live right side up in this upside down world.

Jason Evans, Pastor, Bethel Hill Baptist Church, Bethel Hill, North Carolina

In this compelling book, David Alan Black has done two things at once: he has reminded Baptists of their heritage and provoked Christians to reclaim the gospel as a way of life. These are powerful words because he speaks from his own experience. Written in an engaging style and with great humility, Black has done the Church at large and Baptists in particular a great service: if we heed his words we will recover the way of Christ as the only way to live.

Rodney Reeves, Dean, The Courts Redford College of Theology and Ministry, Southwest Baptist University

I was very pleased to read of David Black's longings for a more pure and passionate following in the footsteps of Jesus and the apostles. He is a maverick and I love mavericks. They usually have something very important to say to "the flock." The church in America has lost its way, and church leadership would do well to listen to his prophetic voice calling for "Body ministry" among all the believers. His strongest points were to challenge the church to serve one another in love, to reach the least and the lost, and to spend one's life discipling them, whatever the cost – even if it be to suffer and to die. He has the attitude of the overcomer in Revelation 12:11, and he isn't afraid to say that he loves not his reputation nor his life even unto death. Very few "church people" talk in that way. Because of his willingness to lay aside everything for Jesus' sake and take up the mantle of humility and suffering, his words can be disarming for those who are in love with this world. He also lives with integrity and dignity, for he honestly seeks to flesh out his "churchology."

L. Smith, pastor's wife

In *The Jesus Paradigm*, Dr. Black articulates the growing concern from both laity and academia that Christianity, particularly in North America, is no longer recognizable as that defined in the New Testament. His critique of various Christian practices, to be sure, is painful to hear yet necessary and calls for a long overdue self-calibration. His invitation to relinquish power and ambition for power is an incisive critique of the Church's misunderstanding of both the cross and discipleship. *The Jesus Paradigm* is a refreshing contribution and worthwhile for any claiming the name of Christ.

M. Sydney Park, Assistant Professor of Divinity, Beeson Divinity School

The Jesus Paradigm

David Alan Black

Energion Publications

P. O. Box 841
Gonzalez, FL 32560

http://energionpubs.com
pubs@energion.com

Cover Image: *Crucifixion*, by Gregory Eanes (gregoryeanes.com)

Crucifixion also used on title page and chapter headings.

ISBN-10: 1-893729-56-7
ISBN-13: 978-1-893729-56-8

Library of Congress Control Number: 2009932212

Dedication

To my wife Becky, whose example of humble service in the name of Jesus has been and always will be for me a plumb line and inspiration.

Darling, your life is a perpetual challenge to me — a challenge to live life more fully and more sacrificially each day, to draw closer to God, to love my family and friends, and to align my priorities according to the way of Jesus.

Thank you. I love you.

CONTENTS

v

Preface

I honestly never thought I'd be writing this book. My idea of life was to get married, have children, teach Greek for forty years, and retire. I never figured I'd be writing a book about what truly makes life worth living – loving, giving, and caring for others. Scripture says, "What advantage is it if you gain the whole world and lose your own soul?"[1] That's a great lesson I've had to learn. It took me a while to understand my purpose in life, but it's finally coming into focus. Whether I'm opening my home to strangers, or showing the Jesus Film in a remote village, or preaching to prisoners, or singing to shut-ins, I now realize that I exist for one reason: to live for Jesus by serving others in his name. I was raised to think that the world exists for me. Now I realize that I exist for the world.

This book is written for anyone who is dissatisfied with cultural Christianity and who longs for a greater reality in the whole Body of Christ. Its plea is that we get serious about following Jesus. It is written for anyone who is ready to build unity around the essentials of Christianity and get on with the top priorities. I draw great courage from the fact that a new generation of Christians is awakening to Jesus' call to a sacrificial lifestyle. I have begun to witness a major paradigm shift from cultural Christianity to radical discipleship. It appears that God is raising up a group of Jesus-followers who understand that regardless of what we believe on secondary and tertiary issues, evangelicals need to start acting like Christians if we are to build the kingdom of God among every people of the world. There seems to be a growing realization that *every* member of Christ's Body needs to be involved in kingdom work, not just paid professionals. This will not happen unless we face our own materialism and even laziness, unless we deliberately choose to live more simply so that others may simply live. I believe it is

---

[1] All translations/paraphrases in this book are my own.

time for repentance from selfish ambition and theological snobbery. Following Christ means taking seriously his call for an exclusive and costly attachment to him. This is because Christianity is not a religion or a denomination or a political organization. It is a new society living out the ethics of the kingdom of God. It is a radical, Christ-centered, martyr movement.

For the record, I am a strong believer in doctrinal purity. Such doctrines as the virgin birth of Jesus, the authenticity of miracles, and the inerrancy of Scripture are non-negotiables for me. I would be the last person to depreciate theology or a proper emphasis on truth. But orthodoxy is incomplete – a disastrous aberration even – without orthopraxy. This book emerged from a movement of God in my heart to go beyond proper belief to a new way of living. Following in the footsteps of Jesus, I have found myself making the Jesus way of life known in the remotest villages of Ethiopia, the poverty-stricken slums of India, the high-rise churches of South Korea, the offices of Muslim clerics in the Middle East, and the local nursing homes and hospitals where I live. Amid all the debates over Calvinism and the King James Version and the emerging church and worship styles I have come to a slightly different realization: that God is calling out a people who are committed to living lives of genuine obedience to Christ, a community of faith that functions in Christ-like ways – visibly, voluntarily, sacrificially – to show people this thing Jesus called the kingdom.

This way of Jesus, this way of the cross, transcends political loyalties. I recognize that this is a controversial statement to make in a nation of "red" and "blue" Christians. I frankly do not expect evangelicals on either end of the political spectrum to be happy with my position. But anyone who tries to make Jesus into a conservative or a liberal must be reading a different Bible than the one I know and love. I believe that the church should be moving away from, not toward, political solutions to the world's problems. The fact that Jesus' kingdom is "not of this world" requires us to distrust *any* political system, including those that claim they can bring peace and justice to the world. Why should we put our faith in systems that belong to the "powerless and bankrupt principles of this world" (Gal. 4:9)? On the contrary, I believe it is time the church transferred its loyalty and citizenship from the kingdoms of the world to the kingdom of God.

Please don't misunderstand me. I'm not denying the need for Christian participation in social service. Jesus' command to "love our neighbor" obviously requires the serving of human need. The danger is the politicization of the church – that is, the temptation for the church to take up a "cause" (non-proliferation, economic equality, environmentalism, demo-cratization, etc.) and then seek to promote "justice" through theological arguments. It is my conviction that only when the church keeps its involvement nonpartisan can it go about its legitimate business of serving humanity. The Christian Gospel cannot be equated with any political movement or cause. Let the Republicans support their faith-based initiatives (that rely on government funding) and the Democrats their welfare programs (that also depend on government funding), but let them do so for political reasons, not for theological ones. Theologically, the only commitment Christians are to have is to be Christ's witnesses, to proclaim his kingdom, and to preach the life-changing Gospel to all who will listen.

I must warn you: this book is not for the timid. Within these pages you will find tough questions and (hopefully) straight answers. I may be wrong, but no one can say I am afraid to speak my mind or to take on hard issues. Of course, it's one thing to talk about radical discipleship, and another thing to practice it. This book tries to bridge the gap between theory and practice. My guess right now is that you're probably wondering if it is even possible. Until I learn differently, I'll offer what I know, with the hope that a passion to follow hard after Jesus will be stirred within you, perhaps even a deeper passion than you've ever known before. It's not going to be easy, but as we take on an attitude of humility and teachability, I believe we can expect to see the Spirit give birth to a powerful new movement of sacrificial service in the North American church.

I'm fortunate enough to be writing this preface on the front porch of my farmhouse in Virginia, surrounded by dense summer foliage and beautifully fragrant flowers. But God didn't bless me with all this so that I could just sit around and watch flowers. Where much is given, much is required, and my blessings have only made me more aware of the millions of people who do not enjoy the blessings I have. I'm far from being the committed Christ-follower that I want to be, but I do believe I've begun traveling the downward path of Jesus.

Care to join me?

Acknowledgments

A bee draws nectar from many flowers. I have benefited richly from several literary blossoms. These are indicated in the footnotes to this book. In addition, several friends have read the manuscript in part or in whole and have offered their constructive criticism: Jason Evans, Chris Jacobs, Ed Johnson, and Kevin Brown. My thanks to each one. I especially want to thank my son Nathan for bringing his sure judgment to bear at crucial junctures. Of course, I am fully responsible for errors and views found in this book.

Thanks also go to Henry Neufeld of Energion Publications for guiding the publication process from inception to birth.

There are many excellent books on discipleship written from the viewpoint of a philosopher or skilled debater. This is not one of them. I don't offer the thoughts of a scholar or theologian. This is a book written out of my own experiences. If it helps you in your own walk with God, may he get all the glory.

The final "thank you" must go to him.

Introduction: The Jesus Paradigm

> Part of the scandal of the gospel is that when you meet the abandoned, crucified Messiah, he grabs you and you belong to him. Wherever you are in privilege and power and status and opportunity, you start down until you are powerless, except for his power; you go down until you find yourself with the riffraff. The evangelists I listened to in my youth didn't make that clear. But the evangelists in the New Testament make that devastatingly clear.
>
> Gordon Cosby[2]

Smashing Our Idols

Power has ruined America. Not only on the liberal left. Now it seems to have done the same for the religious right. The right has a large clientele. When it takes a wrong turn it turns all its followers in the wrong direction. The right has taken over every platitude, every trite slogan. It has prostituted itself with power, status, and wealth. Only a few would deny that these attitudes have infiltrated a large segment of the evangelical church in America. There is only one small light left in the darkness, and it is the pure Word of God. A recovery of the fundamentals is still possible, but only if we read and heed the Scriptures. Here is where the Master's genius is fully revealed. He turns the status grid on its head. Power cannot last if we do not worship it.

---

[2]Cited in Jim Wallis, *Agenda for a Biblical People* (New York: Harper and Row, 1976), 96-97.

I wrote this book because I feel it is urgent that the church in America rediscover the meaning of its existence. Of greatest importance is that we stop viewing the church as an end rather than a means to an end: it is God's means of sculpturing a new race, a spiritual kingdom out of the dross of humanity. Rather than hit-and-run tactics, an inclusive strategy can and must be agreed upon. Speaking as a realist, I know that there will always be a degree of continuity with present patterns of church life, rigid and uncritical though they may be. I am also convinced that pseudo-radical ideas (including some ideas coming out of the emerging church movement) will not work because they have the same clericalism, institutionalism, and status-consciousness as do most conventional churches. It is time for constructive new proposals, and more and more Christians, young and old, are asking what can be done. If the Spirit is willing, and if we act together, change can happen – change for the better, for the advancement of the kingdom, and for the glory of God.

What might this kingdom-focused church of the twenty-first century look like? It will be a serving church. Its organizational structure will be simple, unencumbered by bureaucrats and bureaucracies. Its financial priorities will reflect a commitment to missions, local and global. Capital expenditures will be reduced and the savings earmarked for discipleship. Most jobs that are currently salaried positions will be filled by volunteer help or eliminated. Denominations will make drastic reductions in funds spent on publications that are a waste of the church's money (bulletins, glossy magazines, and Sunday School quarterlies – the Bible will be used instead). Church buildings will be used for primary and secondary Christian education. Believers will gladly work transdenominationally and cooperatively, especially at the local level. The church will proclaim the Good News of the Gospel as its first priority while not neglecting the cultural mandate. A full-fledged lay ministry will replace clericalism. Individual believers will be expected to assume specialized ministries according to their giftedness. Churches will provide regular lay training and build voluntary programs of education into their structures. Worship will no longer be confined to a single time or place. Preoccupation with church buildings will be seen for what it is – idolatry. The church will no longer cling to its prerogatives but take the form of a servant. It will refuse any longer to shun the secular. Trained pastors will become humble assistants to the "ministers" – every member. Disciples will take the going forth as seriously as they do the gathering. New believers will be asked to specify a regular community involvement (neighborhood council, PTA, volunteer library staff, nursing home visitation, etc.) in addition to their commitment to a ministry in the church.

The points I have been making – and I could offer many more examples of positive descriptions of the renewed church – do not represent simply my own opinion. They are backed up by countless studies that contrast sharply with the grandiose structures we have become accustomed to since Christendom came on the scene. The fight of faith to which we are committed is not a battle against Christianity. It is a battle to free Christianity from the shackles of Christendom, to smash our idols, and to establish a church that is once again characterized by poverty of spirit.

Imitating Christ

The truth of the matter is this. Somewhere along the way we lost our biblical moorings. Human models based on anthropology and psychology became the vogue. The world and its "boastful pride of life" lured us into accepting false panaceas. But rather than following the world, we are called to be followers of Jesus. By "followers of Jesus" I do not mean mere admirers of Jesus, but people radically committed to following his example and teachings – a minority group, if you will, within a culture created by Christian majority groups. When I wrote in my book *Paul, Apostle of Weakness*[3] that power is weakness and weakness strength I meant to promote not otherworldly

---

[3] New York: Peter Lang, 1984.

mysticism but the deepest reality of all: that the way up is down, that weakness wins, that the Lamb who was slain is worthy to receive power and might and glory and honor. Had Paul lived four centuries later he no doubt would have been appalled that the persecuted church had entered into an unholy alliance with the dominant political and economic power of the world. Nor do I think he would have found any pleasure in the evolution of Christianity into sacerdotal clericalism at the expense of every-member ministry. Paul called his followers to imitate him – and Christ – in renouncing dominion and in favor of servanthood.

Does this mean that followers of Christ – that this Christian minority within a Christian majority – has nothing to say to the rest of society? Hardly. If I understand the New Testament aright, the church is to take on a nonconformist and prophetic identity over against the structures of the world. This is not to say that I am unconcerned about politics or about the improvement of society through legislation. Such improvements are, however, questionable if they proceed from an assumption that they will issue in a Christian America.[4] My concern is that the church be the church, and to do that it must proclaim victory not through a political agenda but through the Christian Gospel. The Christianity of the New Testament presents not simply a more demanding ethic but rather a cross that means the death of our desire for prosperity and power. I therefore view my participation in the culture wars not in terms of calling for a

---

[4] This is the main thesis of Gregory Boyd's outstanding book, *The Myth of a Christian Nation* (Grand Rapids: Zondervan, 2005), which challenges head-on the widely-held "Christian America" point of view. In spite of whatever criticisms may be leveled at Boyd for his views on open theology (a position with which I strongly disagree), I concur that the religious right's agenda is misguided, even ruinous. See also Randall Balmer, *Thy Kingdom Come: How the Religious Right Distorts the Faith and Threatens America* (New York: Basic Books, 2006). A nation, of course, cannot be "Christian" any more than a chair, since Christianity implies an act of conscious faith.

macro-political utopia but in terms of the church's calling to be
the conscience and critic of culture.[5]

What, then, does it mean to be a disciple of Jesus in today's
world? What it does *not* mean is that we are free from
responsibility in the world – free to sit around and stew, free to
be passive sheep, free to be blind to the sins of nationalism, or
statism, or militarism, or any of the other -isms that plague us.
Nor does it mean that we adopt the stratagem of the Herodians
and the Sadducees of Jesus' day – doing the best we can under
the circumstances, compromising our religious convictions for
political advantage, going along to get along. Neither passive
withdrawal nor pro-establishment politicking will do. It all comes
down to this: if we are to be followers of Jesus we must be salt
and light, we must preach the Good News to the poor, we must
be God's people in the world, putting into practice the different
quality of life that is promised to all who follow him in

---

[5] I have stated this explicitly in the introduction to my website, Dave
Black Online: "As you read my *columns and essays*, you will notice that I
believe many Americans have forsaken the primacy of the cross of
Christ, embracing instead the state as their Savior. They naively follow
the example of the churches in Nazi Germany by placing their faith in
broken-down human hierarchies, forgetting that such edifices are mere
man-made Towers of Babel, be they liberal or conservative, Democrat
or Republican. Politicians of both parties are working tirelessly to
undermine the fundamental principles of religious liberty guaranteed
to 'We the People' in the founding documents of our nation, obsessed
by the foolish notion that what they deem to be evil can be cured by
the federal government. Indeed, the culture of political correctness
has become so institutionalized that most Americans have stopped
opposing it. I believe it is time to stop seeking God in the misguided
and erroneous teachings of do-goodism, whether the source is
liberalism or conservatism. *Jesus Christ is the only answer to the malaise
plaguing our families, our churches, and our society.* You can idolize man-made
institutions with the hope that they will solve the societal ills of our
day if you like, but I prefer to stand by the Bible and the life-changing
power of the cross." See http://daveblackonline.com/welcome.htm.

obedience and love. It means reserving allegiance to Christ and not to any worldly Caesar. "We reject the false doctrine that the Church can and must acknowledge as a source of its proclamation, beside and in addition to this one Word of God, other elements, powers, forms and truths as the revelation of God," asserts the famous *Barmen Declaration* (Article 1), written by members of the Confessing Church in World War II Germany. Barmen is still valid today. Those who are followers of Jesus are set apart from others by their confession of Jesus as Lord (a *political* title!) and their adherence to the one Word of God as their infallible guide.

The Jesus Paradigm

Unlike Hitler's Confessing Church opponents, the religious right in America (or at least a large portion of it) is squarely aligned with the powers that be. I once supported the alliance. Not anymore. Radical disciples of Jesus embrace those on the other side of the dividing walls of hostility in our world, even including our "enemies." Christianity transcends *all* boundaries – cultural, racial, political, geographical, natural, even national. This understanding of Christianity was commonplace in the early church. Only after Constantine did it become a minority position. Even the Reformers continued the church-state alliance. "Christian" warfare continued unabated, and the rise of nation-states only led to its increase.

Thankfully, this attitude is gradually changing. I praise God for the growing number of Jesus-followers who refuse to worship the nation-state and the pervading cultural infatuation with violence, who instead prefer the scandalous way of powerless love, who realize – whether American or Ethiopian or Chinese – that they are a pilgrim people who live in the world and yet have their real citizenship in a kingdom that is both partly present and coming in all its fullness. Unfortunately, many churches are unwilling to change at all. As Brian McLaughlin observes:

The default position of many (most?) churches is that a spiritually formed person will be very involved in the institution of the church (and not the other church across town, but our church!): attend the building. Give money to the building. Serve in the building. Invite people to the building. Do everything for the building. As McNeal summarizes, "we have made following Jesus all about being a good church member." But is this what it means to follow Christ?[6]

There is, I am convinced, a better way. It is what I am calling the "Jesus paradigm." The expression alludes to the way Jesus concluded his earthly ministry. He washed his disciples' feet and then said, "I have given you an example so that you may copy what I have done" (John 13:15). This is the way Jesus sought to glorify his Father. It is the exact opposite of our human way. We seek glory by moving upward. Jesus chose the way of downward mobility, through suffering for us. Whenever he speaks about being glorified – being "lifted up" – he always refers to his death. It was through the cross that Jesus glorified his Father and made known God's glory to us.

Today Jesus is calling his followers to continue his mission of radical, sacrificial love in this world. He wants us to keep nothing for ourselves. He wants us to stoop and touch the places in other people that most need washing. The American church has forgotten this servant role of Christianity. We attempt to exploit the powers rather than persuade them to conform to the way of Christ. We have forgotten that our only loyalty is to be to Christ and not to the state. Read the Gospels and you will arrive at an inescapable conclusion: it is the *suffering* Jesus who is the paradigm of the Christian life. The well-known axiom from Martin Kähler that the Gospels are "passion narratives with extended introductions" clearly applies here. Jesus is the "king

---

[6]http://triangularchristianity.wordpress.com/2008/07/02/the-present-future-return-to-spiritual-formation/.

who didn't reign," in contrast to the false triumphalism found in the Hellenistic tradition of the "divine man" who masters the cosmic forces of evil. The Gospels proclaim "Christ crucified" every bit as much as the apostle Paul does (1 Cor. 2:2). They warn us against the moral distortion that runs rife in our churches. Insofar as the Messiah was understood as a political deliverer, the Gospels are not only apolitical, they are anti-political, for the Christ they present stands in diametrical opposition to the conventional messianic hope of the day.

This "Jesus paradigm" – this downward path I have been describing – offers us a completely alternative vision of the church. The old Christendom model exalts the church *as church*. In Christendom our ultimate identity lies in being "good church goers." It involves "accepting Jesus as our Savior." It means "sound" preaching and believing the "right" doctrines. Our primary concern becomes "doing church right." So if we hold to the right doctrines and preach expositionally and worship in the right way and refrain from evil practices, we are "good Christians." Jesus, on the other hand, came to inaugurate the kingdom of God. In the Jesus paradigm, our ultimate identity lies in being kingdom builders. His kingdom now becomes our focus. Jesus bids us to enter the kingdom and follow him. In this kingdom, denominations and church loyalty ultimately mean nothing. His was never a kingdom of earthly power, status, and influence to begin with. Moreover, when we enter this kingdom we are brought under his new covenant. In Christ we become new creatures (2 Cor. 5:17). Our lives are transformed by the Spirit of God (Rom. 12:2). We are raised with Christ to walk in newness of life (Rom. 6:4). Crucified with Christ, we now follow in his footsteps (Gal. 2:20; 1 John 2:6). We are servants of righteousness, and the peace of Christ rules in our hearts (Rom. 6:11; Col 3:15). Our lives bear the fruit of Christ's Spirit: love, joy, peace, patience, kindness, goodness, faithfulness, meekness, self-control (Gal. 5:22). We gladly suffer for the cause of Christ, knowing that he suffered and left us an example that we should follow in his steps (1 Pet. 1:10-14; 2:20-21). Our one goal is to live as good citizens of heaven in a manner worthy of the Gospel (Phil. 1:27). We seek to be blameless and harmless before the world, the children of God, without rebuke, in the midst of a crooked and perverse nation (Phil. 2:14-15). We live peacefully with all people and render no one evil for evil (Rom. 12:17-21). We seek first the kingdom of God and his righteousness (Matt. 6:33).

This is the picture of the Christian that one finds in the pages of the New Testament. Far from being merely "good church goers" and passive pew-sitters, followers of Jesus manifest a new quality of life that is enabled and sustained by the Holy Spirit. Its model is the perfect humanity of Jesus Christ, especially his servanthood and cross. This same Jesus, now risen and exalted, has gifted and called all believers to the Christian ministry. This ministry is more than "church work" as we know it. In fact, the church is not a human organization at all.[7] It is called to embody the crucified and resurrected Christ by ministering to the world in the power of the Spirit of God. It is a brotherhood that shares a common vision and willingness to commit itself to a radically new lifestyle that often puts it in jeopardy with the

---

[7] Donald Kraybill observes (*The Upside-Down Kingdom* [Scottsdale, PA: Herald, 2003], 68-69):

> [Jesus] didn't completely spurn established religion. He taught in synagogues and in the temple. He endorsed the Torah…. But when religious practices grew stale he turned them upside-down and inside out and called them back to their original purpose. He refused to bless religious structures, which ranked people by their pious deeds. He replaced the machinery of formalized religion with compassion and love. Jesus, the upside-down Messiah, would become the new high priest. God's Spirit would vacate the Holy of Holies in the temple and abide in the heart of each believer. No longer would people worship God in the holy temple or on a sacred mountain. Now they could approach God anywhere in spirit and in truth.

"principalities and powers." It is a community of grace that functions as an agent of God's love in the world. Humility and sacrifice for the sake of the kingdom are its greatest virtues. Living what is believed is no longer optional.

A Cruciform Lifestyle

To put the matter another way: the Jesus paradigm is cruciform. By "cruciform" I mean that the cross is the hermeneutical key to understanding the revelation of God in Christ. It is this cross that we find so offensive today. The "crucified God" stands in judgment on America's *theologia gloriae* – a "theology of glory" paralleled in Peter's protest against Jesus' passion in Mark 8:32, with its overtones of ethnic triumphalism. Mark's Gospel soberly recognizes where Christ stands with respect to the structures of power, whether in Jerusalem or Rome – or the United States. The only question for the church is: Are we willing to follow Jesus "beyond politics," that is, beyond the cultural optimism that encourages us to think that the most serious problem in the world today is the lack of U.S.-style democracy and a free-market economy? Americans legitimately cherish the greatness of their homeland, but many do not realize how deeply America's foreign policy and international image have been affected by the views of a small group of religious and political conservatives. To speak quite frankly, I have come to deplore the stand that far too many of our politicians have taken in their desire to create through military force a dominant American empire throughout the world. I loathe their contempt for true democracy, their dismissal of elementary human rights, their commitment to global hegemony, their arrogance, militarism, and adventurism, their contempt for international law, their appeal to national security to justify the use of violence. Today the same war drums are beating to rouse public enthusiasm for an attack on Iran – all under the cloak of moralistic righteousness. Acting preemptively has become the new norm in foreign relations. Force reigns supreme in America, and we will exercise that force whenever it is in the "national interest." Even among my fellow evangelicals there is no shortage of elevated ideals to accompany the resort to violence.[8]

Such hubris is inexcusable. It can lead only to disaster. If Iraq is the U.S. exemplar for countering Islamic fundamentalism, then heaven help us. Things are not much different in the church. Like the twelve apostles who consistently misunderstood Jesus, church leaders today often aspire to build their own earthly kingdoms in which "bigger and better" reputations, salaries, and budgets reign. But the New Testament characterizes leadership as "bottom-up" authority – an authority that acknowledges Jesus Christ as the sole Head of the church and that always emphasizes servanthood protection of that great truth through the equal priesthood of all believers. This pattern is set forth for us in the mystery of the Triune God, which provides the example of Christian unity. The first man Adam set the stage for the Great Human Tragedy by failing to submit himself to the Trinity and by "grasping" after what was not rightfully his. The Last Adam, however, has reversed the course of human history by refusing to exploit what was rightly his. The "Good News" of the Gospel is precisely that the saving work of Christ provides not only the forgiving and saving grace of God but also God's transforming and sanctifying grace that is mediated through God's Word and Spirit. Jesus brought into existence a new social

---

[8] One notable exception is David P. Gushee. Gushee is the former Graves Professor of Moral Philosophy and Senior Fellow of the Center for Christian Leadership at Union University. He currently serves as Distinguished University Professor of Christian Ethics at McAfee School of Theology at Mercer University. See esp. his *The Future of Faith in American Politics: The Public Witness of the Evangelical Center* (Waco: Baylor University Press, 2008), in which he calls Christians of all political stripes to follow Jesus without aligning themselves uncritically with either the left or the right. Along similar lines, Gushee has also written *Kingdom Ethics: Following Jesus in Contemporary Context* (Downers Grove: InterVarsity, 2003).

reality in which the actual Person of Christ becomes as important as established theological positions about Christ. Indeed, the New Testament announces the most radical political thought ever to strike the human mind: *the astounding power of spiritual poverty.* We see this theme at the very beginning of the New Testament record, where Matthew offends the patriarchal concepts of his contemporaries by including four "irregular" women in the genealogy of Jesus. This text (Matt. 1:3-6) shows us how the idea of universal chosenness works – how Jesus chooses the inadequate, the weak, the poor, the sinner, the outsider – thus illuminating the power of poverty. For unless we become "poor in spirit" (Matt. 5:3), our riches become our hell. So from the very beginning, the New Testament breathes impoverished air. To deny our poverty is to deny the Christian faith.

This fundamental theme is found also in Paul's magnificent writings, where weakness becomes strength, down becomes up, and poverty becomes wealth. Look at the way he develops this concept into a major theological concept in his letters. Because of the false accusations of his opponents, Paul elevates poverty of spirit into a badge of honor and the chief evidence of his apostolic authority.[9] Paul's concept of servant-leadership is problematic unless we understand that the apostle accepted the hierarchical notions of his day but radically redefined them.[10] There is an implied contradiction, of course, in saying that leaders are servants, but the painful paradox is precisely what the

---

[9] See my *Paul, Apostle of Weakness.*

[10] Paul's concept of servant-leadership was consistent with his own missionary practice, which "derives from the example and the teaching of Jesus himself. ... His motto of revolutionary subordination, of willing servanthood in the place of domination, enables the person in a subordinate position in society to accept and live within that status without resentment, at the same time that it calls upon the person in the superordinate position to forsake or renounce all domineering use of his status" (John H. Yoder, *The Politics of Jesus* [Grand Rapids: Eerdmans, 1972], 190).

New Testament teaches and the early church practiced. As we read the New Testament, we become aware that God delights in taking unimportant nobodies, filling them with his Presence, and empowering them to live lives of sacrificial love (Rom. 12:9-21).

Making Disciples

This brings us back to where we started. Making disciples of Jesus is not very difficult. No fancy programs are necessary. We just have to teach them to do *everything* Jesus said. Being a disciple is simply understanding what Jesus wants and then deciding to do it. And success can be seen when our deeds and words start to naturally look like Christ's. This is one of the undergirding themes of K. P. Yohannan in his book *The Road to Reality*:

> Since when has obedience to Christ and His Gospel become optional to Christianity? What kind of church, culture or ethnic group can produce a faith where obedience to God has become dispensable? We modern Christians have divorced what we do from who we are. More than 50 million Americans have become what is mistakenly called "born again." By this they mean they have walked the aisle to be saved from hell, find peace and joy, escape from guilt, please family and friends, find wealth, health and happiness, and get the preacher off their backs! But a religion measured in such superficial, external terms bears no resemblance to the faith of Scripture.
>
> Jesus is "cool" now in North America. Being a Christian is a respectable, acceptable, and normal choice. What's more, it's free, instant, a convenience-store item. All that is necessary is to pray a 30-word prayer, sign a little card, or put your hand on the TV screen and you're in!

This modern Christianity is weak on the Gospels. You rarely hear an evangelist preach from Matthew, Mark, or Luke. To do so would mean that the ego demands of Christ on His followers would have to become a central concern.

Thus, the false religion of popular Christianity does not ask us to internalize the passion and mind of Christ, to surrender our egos, lay aside our flesh, take up the cross and begin a lifestyle marked by submission to the will of the Father as He did.

We are also seldom asked to internalize the commands of Christ – to begin a lifestyle of sacrifice, service, and suffering for the sake of our Lord.[11]

I write hoping to find more fellow travelers who share a desire to "begin a lifestyle of sacrifice, service, and suffering for the sake of our Lord." I am not minimizing the importance of sound doctrine. But it is not sufficient for us merely to espouse the right doctrines or to feel good about ourselves because we have been saved. The Jesus paradigm requires that we lead a radically new kind of life.

---

[11] K. P. Yohannan, *The Road to Reality* (Carrollton, TX: GFA Books, 1988), 25-26.

The Liberated Church: Recasting Our Vision of Discipleship

The Church is the Church only when it exists for others. To make a start, it would give away all its property to those in need. The clergy must live solely on the free-will offerings of their congregations, or possibly engage in some secular calling. The Church must share in the secular problems of ordinary human life, not dominating, but helping and serving. It must tell men of every calling what it means to live for Christ, to exist for others.

Dietrich Bonhoeffer[12]

Cultural Christianity or Costly Discipleship?

How does one follow Jesus unreservedly in the twenty-first century? That is the central question I am posing in this book.

Let me offer a concrete example. In 1 Corinthians 14 Paul says that in the gathered meeting of the church there should be a time and place for all to bring to the assembly their abilities and

---

[12] *Letters and Papers from Prison*, rev. trans. (New York: Macmillan, 1967), 211.

to contribute their gifts and insights to those assembled. Why, then, is this rarely if ever practiced in our church gatherings, whether in America or abroad?

The first reason, I think, is biblical ignorance. Church leaders, even those who are seminary trained, are often unaware of this scriptural teaching and pattern. There is something profoundly disturbing about such ignorance. Thanks in no small part to the over-intellectualizing of the classroom, many seminary graduates can tell you everything about the New Testament – canonicity, authorship, the synoptic problem – but cannot tell you what it teaches about the church. For the masses of nominal Christians today, the concept of "church" hardly goes beyond a shallow socializing. But the idea of fellowship is not to be trivialized into a spectator event where people expect entertainment and fun. There is to be profound engagement with each other and a joint effort to edify the whole Body. As Howard Snyder has written, "The church has a shortage of 'ministers' only when it fails to see all believers as ministers and thus fails to disciple all believers into leaders."[13] The Anabaptist radicals of the sixteenth century were savvy to all of this, and they solved the problem by emphasizing the authority of being and gifting more than the authority of office and power.[14]

---

[13] *Liberating the Church* (Downers Grove: InterVarsity, 1983), 247.

[14] According to the "Report of the Findings Committee Conference on the Concept of the Believers' Church," held at the Southern Baptist Theological Seminary in 1967, "Every believer participates in the full ministry of Christ. Every believer is a priest, every believer is a prophet or preacher. Every believer participates in that servanthood which Jesus revealed as the mode of His rule. Every believer is endowed with a gift, the exercise of which is essential to the welfare of the body. We reject the concept of ministry as a unique sacramental, professional, or governing caste, and the concept of 'laity' as usually defined negatively from that perspective" (James Leo Garrett, Jr., ed., *The Concept of the Believers' Church* [Scottsdale, PA: Herald, 1969]). If this report accurately represents Anabaptist/Baptist thinking, then one would assume that Baptist churches would conform to the pattern of every-member ministry. But this is hardly the case.

In the second place, the concept of highly participatory meetings of the kind described in 1 Corinthians 14 goes against the grain of long-held ecclesiastical traditions. In fact, "We've never done it this way" is a rallying slogan heard often in many churches. This is nothing less than idolatry, in this case the worship of tradition. A correct reading of the Bible is always countercultural. It always challenges the dominant culture, sometimes even the dominant church culture. Once again, the Anabaptists' emphasis on costly discipleship, on living the Christian life, on the church as a kingdom of priests and ministers, is a healthy antidote to our modern preoccupation with ease and entertainment. In our consumerist, individualistic age, our "worship services" can become simply another excuse for creating barriers and divisions among people instead of a genuine communion with fellow pilgrims on the way. Little wonder Kierkegaard wrote:

> The established church is far more dangerous to Christianity than any heresy or schism. We play at Christianity. We use all the orthodox Christian terminology – but everything, everything without character.... There is something frightful in the fact that the most dangerous thing of all, playing at Christianity, is never included in the list of heresies or schisms.[15]

I don't mean to suggest that there is always a simple way to describe the meeting of a truly New Testament church. Biblically speaking, New Testament ecclesiology is much more than "doing church right." Yet if we are to be true to the New Testament vision of the church as the Body of Christ, we must insist upon a more costly and participatory manifestation of the unity and diversity of Christ's' Body. *We are to be a people committed to mutual service, even costly service.* By adhering to Scripture as the

---

[15] Søren Kierkegaard, *Provocations: Spiritual Writings of Kierkegaard,* ed. Charles E. Moore (Farmington, PA: Plough, 1999), 227.

principal ground of all truth and knowledge, I believe we may expect the Spirit of God to guide an obedient congregation into the use of its manifold giftedness.[16]

How, then, can we recapture today the New Testament emphasis on costly, participatory discipleship? It seems to me that we need, first and foremost, a new definition of "success." Like all institutions, the church is reluctant to change because it has sacralized itself. Our image of a successful church is one that incorporates a hard-working paid staff, a large and expanding membership, a growing budget, and a multiplicity of programs. The "laity," if they act at all, largely function as assistants to the paid clergy in church activities. The patterns we are led to in the book of Acts indicate a vastly different focus, form, and function. *The church is simply a group of radical Jesus-followers ministering to each other sacrificially and reaching the community about them with the Gospel in word and deed.*[17] Never in the New Testament do we see the pastor as the "key man" upon whom rests the burden of speaking for the Body in a way that no other person can. Jesus not only taught but practiced involvement, and so must we. This is why the Anabaptists emphasized again and again the necessary link between the new birth and the life of the newborn Christian. Regeneration is more than a positional truth. It is more than the forgiveness of sins. It is a quest for obedience and self-sacrifice and thus the very opposite of Protestant scholasticism.

This kind of radical discipleship as taught by Jesus and modeled for us by the early church is, I am convinced, the great need of the hour. Avery Dulles, writing about the contemporary church in America, observes:

---

[16] In chapter 4, I discuss the concept of communal ecclesiology in greater detail.
[17] See Matt. 28:19-20; Acts 2:42-47; Rom. 12:9-21; Eph. 4:17-5:2; Phil. 2:1-16.

It is clear today ... that convinced Christians are a minority in nearly every country ... including nominally Christian and Catholic nations. In our own country we are coming to a fuller awareness that a response to the call of Jesus is both personal and demanding.... To be disciples of Jesus requires that we continually go beyond where we are now. To obey the call of Jesus means separating ourselves from all attachments and affiliations that could prevent us from hearing and following our authentic vocation. To set out on a road to discipleship is to dispose oneself for a share in the cross (cf. Jn. 16:20). To be a Christian, according to the New Testament, is not simply to believe with one's mind, but also to become a doer of the word, a wayfarer with and witness to Jesus. This means, of course, that we never expect complete success within history and that we must regard as normal even the path of persecution and the possibility of martyrdom.[18]

The earliest followers of Jesus insisted that disciples prioritize God's kingdom rather than worldly self-seeking, even if that meant their martyrdom. They taught that "Jesus is Lord," far from being a meaningless catchphrase, is a radical claim. For them, Christianity was incompatible with allegiance to other authorities, be they political, cultural, or ethnic. To put the matter another way: If a community of Christ-followers is to maintain vitality over a long period of time, structures that prevent radical discipleship must be identified and amended accordingly. Where I live and work in the southeastern United States, the Gospel has long been tied to a cultural Christianity that finds it very easy to

---

[18] Avery Dulles, as cited in Jane Elyse Russell, "Love Your Enemies: The Church as Community of Nonviolence," *The Wisdom of the Cross*, eds. Stanley Hauerwas, Chris K. Huebner, Harry J. Huebner, Mark Thiessen Nation (Grand Rapids: Eerdmans, 1999), 386.

compartmentalize faith. NASCAR, divorce, flag-waving, and "Victory in Jesus" appear as one and the same thing, so subtly has compromise been woven into the fabric of the post-bellum South. How, I wonder, can it be so easy to claim the lordship of Jesus Christ and yet so easy to set aside the call to radical obedience to the same Lord? Have we become so blinded by unredeemed cultural forces that we are no longer aware how frequently and systematically we fail to bring all things under the lordship of Christ?

Christendom or Christ?

A scholar for whom such questions of ultimate allegiance are more than academic is Jacque Ellul, a profoundly insightful thinker whose works are well worth reading. Ellul is a classic example of a theologian who asks how our ecclesiological viewpoints have been shaped by tradition rather than by Scripture.[19] He locates the great shift from biblical Christianity to "Christendom" in the rise of Constantine and in the subsequent alliance between church and empire. Christendom represented not a victory for the church but its fall, argues Ellul. Discipleship was replaced with ritual, every-member ministry with a hierarchy that protects "orthodoxy." Seeking first and only the kingdom of God gave way to a Christianity without Christ.

Perhaps it is this "Christless Christianity" that makes me feel so out of step with southern churchianity. At times I even find myself looking at it like an unbeliever who wonders what all the excitement is about. The call of the Gospel has become something radical in my life. It is no longer acceptable for me to "do church." I seek, and have been seeking, a thoroughgoing conversion of every realm of my life, including politics, economics, missions, and personal relationships. Being a citizen

---

[19] See esp. his *The Presence of the Kingdom* (New York: Seabury, 1967), *The Politics of God and the Politics of Man* (Grand Rapids: Eerdmans, 1972), and *The Subversion of Christianity* (Grand Rapids: Eerdmans, 1986).

of God's kingdom involves a commitment to a radical way of living that both rejects the corrosive influences of Christendom and embraces a citizenship status quite apart from political or official church structures in any given time or place. This is why I am so attracted to the Anabaptists of the sixteenth century. For them, Christian discipleship meant trading *everything* for the privilege of gathering voluntarily around the person and example of Christ and of giving all for the cause of Christ's mission in the world. Restoration, not reformation, was their goal. "The reformers aimed to reform the old Church by the Bible; the radicals attempted to build a new church from the Bible."[20] These "brethren," as they preferred to call themselves, were committed to true Christian brotherhood and to keeping the commandments of Christ, even if that meant death. To put it another way, the heart of the Anabaptist vision was not in its ecclesiology but in its soteriology. They taught that regeneration by the Holy Spirit, if indeed genuine, always leads to visible obedience and radical discipleship.

I now realize that the "simple" questions I began asking about ecclesiology eight years ago required a fuller response than I had expected. I needed to relearn the central place of Spirit-enabled obedience in the Christian life. During my career as a professor in several Christian institutions, much was indeed said about radical discipleship. But the highly nuanced Christian jargon used, even at the seminary level, made spiritual and theological language sound irrelevant, superficial, and even offensive. The Anabaptists greatest gift to the church, as I see it, was their ability to cut to the core of our problem as Christians: *our refusal to repudiate churchianity and to be radically committed to Jesus as Lord.* They were prepared to pay any price necessary to develop churches dedicated exclusively to faith and life under biblical authority. When the young Swiss and German Anabaptists produced the Schleitheim Confession in 1527, they

---

[20] Phillip Schaff, cited in R. J. Smithson, *The Anabaptists* (London: James Clarke & Co., 1935), 14-15.

made clear their conviction that any involvement of the magistrate in the life of the church was an unacceptable compromise. How could they have known that Michael Sattler, a former Benedictine monk who bore primary responsibility for drafting the confession, would shortly thereafter be burned at the stake, with his wife being executed by drowning two days later? I too am finding that the struggle to be radically obedient can be a very difficult road. Every time I pray I feel the struggle. It is a struggle of letting Jesus be the Lord of my whole being, of finding true freedom in enslavement and complete surrender to him. I cannot come to Christ with just half my being. God's love is a jealous love. He wants not just a part of me, but all of me.

Two Allegiances?

But there is more than this at stake. As I write this chapter I am in Bahir Dar, Ethiopia, 6,000 miles from my home in Virginia. During my foreign trips I often think about America and wonder if we are nearing the end of Christianity in the United States. The dysfunction of our institutionalized churches seems all too obvious to me. At the same time I realize that Christendom will not die without a desperate struggle. Where I live, churchianity continues to be a very satisfactory mode of operation. Add to this the power and lure of wealth, success, and political influence, and you have an evangelical church that has every reason to maintain the status quo and squelch dissent. And now we are faced in America with an ascendant right-wing political movement that blindly supports the nation-state's empire-building and its propagation of "democracy" (the latest idol in the American pantheon) by means of cruise missiles. It is a well-documented fact[21] that the reigning doctrine of U.S. military preemption owes its existence in large part to the

---

[21] See, e.g., Kevin Phillips, *American Theocracy* (New York: Penguin, 2007) and Craig Unger, *The Fall of the House of Bush* (New York: Scribner, 2007), especially chapter 2 ("Redeemer Nation").

espousal of the just war tradition by conservative, Bible-believing evangelicals. "We wage war to save civilization itself,"[22] asserted a heady George W. Bush on November 8, 2001, even as the evangelical right was gearing up to support Bush's prosecution of our invasions of Afghanistan and Iraq without congressional declarations of war (as required by the United States Constitution). Just as egregious is the now widely accepted notion that political ends justify whatever means are necessary to accomplish them, including disinformation campaigns designed to win public support for our military adventures abroad.

Ruminating on these matters makes me aware of just how fragmented my own life has been so far. Peter Maurin reminds us that we should be "announcers" and not merely "denouncers." "Don't criticize what is not being done. Find the work you can perform, fit yourself to perform it, and then do it."[23] What can a 57-year old professor of ancient Greek do to make a positive contribution to Christ's kingdom? Over the past few years I have gradually come to know the joy of caring for my less fortunate brothers and sisters in the world, especially in Ethiopia. But it is not enough to do deeds of service to others. Jesus did not say, "Blessed are those who help the poor," but "Blessed are the poor." Jesus invites us to *be* poor, and that is much harder than serving the poor. The downward path of Jesus is a way of spiritual poverty – a *consistent* lifestyle of sacrificial service rather than occasional acts of solidarity with people who cannot give us anything. We are called to be revolutionaries in society by following the Jesus paradigm. Our only loyalty should be to him and the kingdom he is building. We cannot have two masters. We cannot have two allegiances. We cannot serve two kingdoms.

---

[22] http://www.strategicstudiesinstitute.army.mil/ksil/files/00097.doc.
[23] Cited in Lee Griffith, *The War on Terrorism and the Terror of God* (Grand Rapids: Eerdmans, 2002), 260.

Lions or Lambs?

Why, then, do we remain so divided in our loyalties? Is our problem ignorance or indifference? Or is it outright disobedience?

As a seminary professor, I have often struggled with this issue. My spirit is needled by questions like these: Is there really a point to theology? Are there any signs that all of our theologizing makes any difference in our lives? Is there anything to hope for after we have mastered the essentials of Christology, Pneumatology, Eschatology, etc.? These questions, for me, are far from speculative. They touch the very core of my Christian life and my work as a teacher. The issue is best posed as follows: *Is the evangelical church in America prepared to deal with biblical truth, not just on the intellectual level, but on the level of daily living?* I sometimes think that our courses in theology and church history and Greek and Hebrew do more to distract us than to deepen our sense of mission. Both theological conservatives and theological liberals are, I think, in constant danger of becoming completely irrelevant. Jim Cymbala's comment is important:

> Let me make a bold statement. Christianity is not predominantly a teaching religion. We have been almost overrun by the cult of the speaker .... It is fine to explain *about* God, but far too few people today are experiencing the living Christ in their lives. We are not seeing God's visitation in our gatherings. We are not on the lookout for his outstretched hand.
>
> The teaching of doctrine is a prelude, if you will, to the supernatural.[24]

---

[24] Jim Cymbala, *Fresh Wind, Fresh Fire: What Happens When God's Spirit Invades the Hearts of His People* (Grand Rapids: Zondervan, 1997), 151-52.

Again, the Anabaptists provide a good model for us to consider. For them, the Body of Christ was the practical extension of the incarnation of its Head *by every individual member*, educated or uneducated. By contrast, Luther and Calvin saw the solidarity between Jesus and his followers in the offices of the church rather than in the lives of every member. The true church, for them, is one where the Word is correctly preached and the sacraments properly administered. These assumptions I find nowhere in the New Testament.[25] Theology is a practical discipline to be engaged in not only by academic professionals but by all true disciples. Paul's vision of church life, as we have noted already, entails Christians being involved with each other in mutual service, help, and support. Passivity and spectatorism are simply never envisioned by the apostle. According to Matthew 28:19-20, the first concern of theological education is to be mission at the local church level and mission that affects obedience to *all* of Jesus' commands. Otherwise, theology will remain a square peg in a round hole. The type of contextualized theology that I am speaking of does not permit a split between academy and church, between thought and action, between truth and practice. Missions lies at the heart of the theological endeavor. Yet our theological curriculum, ostensibly designed to teach us to minister as Jesus and his apostles did, tends to ignore this vital dimension. It is perhaps unfortunate that "missions" has become firmly established as a theological specialization in our seminaries. Dealing with missions is a "must" in *every* theological curriculum.

Suffice it to say that, if we accept the concept of every-member ministry, we will no longer accept biblical teaching that

---

[25]Writes Howard A. Snyder, *The Community of the King* (Downers Grove: InterVarsity, 2004), 38, n. 11: "Neither Luther nor Calvin saw the church as identical with the state or with society in general. They even admitted a certain tension between the church and society. But they did not conceive the church as a sociologically distinct, self-conscious community existing in evident tension with the surrounding society, that is, as a counterculture."

is divorced from meaningful service to others. Christianity is a movement, not a system or organization. If there is to be any organization, it is to be decentralized and flexible, based on a volunteerist theology. Lay empowerment must play a central role. This means that we would return to ministry structures that are supported voluntarily by congregations. Top-heavy denominational structures that siphon off resources to pay for facilities and executive salaries would be replaced by local church ministries, for there is no higher or more strategic locus of God's work on earth than the local communities of God's people. The key to church renewal is very simple: *every follower of Jesus is to live what is believed.* Doctrine should always lead to discipleship, regardless of the personal costs. Jim Elliott, who was martyred for his faith and not only taught but practiced the downward path of Jesus, put it well:

> Systematic theology, be careful how you tie down the Word of God to fit your set and final creeds, systems, dogmas, and organized theistic philosophies. The Word of God is not bound! It's free to say what it will to the individual, and no one can outline it into dispensations which cannot be broken. Don't get it down "cold" but let it live, fresh, warm, and vibrant, so that the world is not binding ponderous books about it, but rather it is shackling you for having allowed it to have full course in your life.[26]

I pray that a new kind of church will emerge in the twenty-first century, one that again asserts that the main task of theology is the formation of loyal disciples of God's way, a community of believers in Jesus committed to service and, when necessary, to suffering and death. This commitment will not condemn materialism in the world while condoning careerism in its own leadership. It will not prate about the evils of the welfare

---

[26] *The Journals of Jim Elliott* (Grand Rapids: Revell, 2002), 14.

state while denying the importance of volunteerism and personal responsibility in its own life. Its fellowship will be truly communal in nature and characterized neither by rampant individualism nor by ecclesiastical legalism. It will recover what was basic about the church before "the pride of the hierarchs, the arrogance of the professional theologians, and the ambitions of temporal rulers had enhanced its outward show of prestige and weakened its true inward strength."[27] The kingdom of heaven, said Jesus, belongs to those who are poor in spirit, to those who love their enemies, to those who refuse retaliation when wronged, to those who accept his rightful reign. This kingdom belongs especially to those who walk in Spirit-obedience to the way of Christ, who follow in the steps of the one "who, because he existed in the form of God, did not consider equality with God something to be exploited, but emptied himself" (Phil. 2:6-7). This is the "offense of the cross" that the apostle Paul spoke of so often – a crucified Messiah, a God-man who refused empire-building and power-broking, a Christ who responded to injustice and violence with self-giving love. "Just try to imagine that the Pattern is called a 'Lamb,'" wrote Kierkegaard. "That alone is a scandal to the natural mind. Who has any desire to be a lamb?"[28]

This is precisely my point of concern. It is relatively easy to follow Jesus *to* the cross, but it is considerably more difficult to follow him *on* the cross. The reason is clear: We want to be lions, not lambs. We invest our lives and our hearts in building our own kingdoms (our churches and ministries) instead of the kingdom of God. It is success, we say, that is the wisdom of God, not the cross. This eclipse of a kingdom-mindset is nothing less than tragic. Let anyone who thinks that radical obedience is not needed in today's world come with me to Armenia or India or Ukraine and see the poverty and smell the dung and hear the crying of the people. Let those who

---

[27] Franklin Little, *A Tribute to Menno Simons* (Scottsdale, PA: Herald, 1961), 24.

[28] *Provocations*, 236.

champion upward mobility rather than the way of suffering love spend one week with me among the Burjis or the Gujis or the Alabas or the Amharas of Ethiopia. No, the Gospel of Jesus Christ is not equivalent to the "good life" of Western civilization. Indeed, the opposite is true: it alone offers a real-world alternative to the grasping and getting of American culture.

Only servanthood and love are forces strong enough to break the grip of human sin. The cross alone frees us to serve the needs of all sinners. Christ came not to be served but to serve. To be greatest, Jesus took the last place on earth. His followers must also be prepared to reject the ways of might and dominion so prevalent among the powerful of our day. As we follow Jesus, he patiently teaches us to deny ourselves as he did in the service of others. Even if we lose our lives in servanthood, we are promised that this self-denial will yield ultimate blessing. Jesus never allowed himself to be manipulated. Yet he did allow himself to be victimized by unregenerate worldly powers. Why? To display the dignity of the servanthood to which the Gospel calls all of us.

In responding to Jesus' call to follow him, I must ask myself what it is I can do to get serious about kingdom-focused living. Am I really willing to seek the lower place at the table rather than the place of preeminence and respectability (Luke 14:1-11)? Am I really willing to give to the poor out of my abundance (Luke 19:8)? Am I really willing to touch sinners (Luke 7:36-39)? Am I really willing to proactively use my possessions for the good of God's kingdom (Luke 6:38)? Everything in me balks at this kind of love and sacrifice. I recoil at the thought of forsaking the world and its values – whether religious, political, social, educational, or vocational. To be "sentenced to death," to become "a spectacle to the world," to be "fools for Christ's sake," to be "held in disrepute," to go "hungry and thirsty," to be "poorly clothed," "persecuted," "slandered," "the rubbish of the world," "the dregs of all things" – the apostle Paul might endure such suffering (1 Cor. 4:8-13), or maybe Ethiopian Christians.

But I, Lord? Yet if I, as a Christian, do not practice what I preach, if I continue to major in the minors, if "poor in spirit" remains but a meaningless platitude in my own life, then I am merely an admirer of Jesus and not a true follower.

The End of Christendom?

In the past few decades I have watched the evangelical church in America deteriorate as it was compromised by unbiblical traditions and practices. I have watched our churches embrace a pragmatism that would have been shocking to the earliest Christians in the book of Acts. I have looked on as the moral and constitutional tenets of our nation's Founders were trashed by the infiltration of a statist, Constantinian mindset in many of our denominations. The religion of our age is utopian pragmatism, and with it the whole social structure of America is tumbling down, dethroning its God and undermining all its certainties. I have no doubt that had C. S. Lewis lived long enough he would have devoted another *Screwtape Letter* to the devilish ways the American church has deceived itself into thinking it is following the blueprint of Scripture.

Paradoxically, all of this is being done in the name of progress and prosperity. This tragic development should be signalized by wearing black and flying flags at half mast, but instead we have become more and more zealous in our pursuit of false utopias of every kind, whatever their ideology may be. The prevailing impression I have of the contemporary scene is of an ever-widening chasm between the church of the New Testament and the modern, success-driven fantasy. In his lectures entitled *The End of Christendom*, Malcolm Muggeridge may have had this chasm in mind when he distinguished between Christianity and Christendom. He wrote: "The founder of Christianity was, of course, Christ. The founder of Christendom I suppose could be named as the Emperor Constantine. I believe … that it is not Christ's Christianity which is now floundering. You might even say that Christ himself abolished Christendom before it began by stating that his kingdom was not of this world – one of the most far reaching and important of all his statements."[29]

I agree. With Muggeridge, I would say that Christendom is over but Christ is not, and in that reality lies the promise of the church. Thanks to the great mercy of God and the marvel of Pentecost, the church can be transformed from the sad parody of Christianity it has become into the glorious Bride that God intends for it to be. We need not despair to be living in a time when we have lost the simplicity and purity of the early church. For it is in the very darkest of times – when the church is drowning in the folly of worldly power, fortune, and success – that Christ's light shines brightest. It depends entirely on whether the churches remain true to the teaching of Christ, whether they truly expound his Gospel, and whether they truly heed his Word. If they do, then clearly they will thrive once again, even though in many aspects they may have to die to themselves.

Reformation, Revival, or Restoration?

We return, then, to the question of Christ's new covenant ministry in all of its aspects. How exactly does he work to restore the church to its original purity? There are different answers to this question, and my final step in this chapter is to sketch them.

First, there is the Roman Catholic approach to renewal, an approach that has always fascinated me, not least since I made a systematic study of the theology of Hans Küng during my student days at the University of Basel in the early 1980s. Indeed, one of the most significant renewal movements in the twentieth century (along with the church growth movement, the charismatic movement, and the ecumenical movement) was the emphasis in Catholicism to bring the church up-to-date in order

---

[29] Malcolm Muggeridge, *The End of Christendom* (Grand Rapids: Eerdmans, 1980), 13-14.

to face and answer the challenges of modern society. Since Vatican II (1963-1965) this movement has been called *aggiornamento*, a term that emphasizes the need for the church to keep pace with a rapidly changing world.

In the Protestant world in which I live and work our favorite words for church renewal have been "reformation" and "revival." We might say that the former term is preferred by the Reformed churches, while the latter term characterizes the emphasis found in baptistic and charismatic congregations. Both are appropriate expressions to characterize the work of God in our times. If there is a difference between them, it is one of emphasis only: "reformation" accentuates the Word of God, while "revival" highlights the Spirit of God. A major concern of the contemporary "emerging church" phenomenon, it seems to me, goes beyond reformation and revivalist strategies by emphasizing the "missional" aspect of the church's life.

Here, then, are several strains within the modern church that stress a particular aspect of ecclesiastical renewal. There is another way to view renewal, however, one that combines what is true in several other renewal movements and that recognizes we have a fundamental responsibility to return to the teaching of the New Testament in both our faith and practice. This is the *church restoration movement*, by which is meant that the church's task is one of returning to the teachings of the apostles in our ecclesiology. Nobody has exemplified the meaning of fidelity to apostolic patterns of church life better than Paul himself:

> I encourage you to imitate me. That's why I'm sending to you Timothy, my son whom I love, who is faithful in the Lord. He will remind you of my way of life in Christ Jesus, which agrees with what I teach everywhere in every church (1 Cor. 4:16-17).

> Imitate me, as I imitate Christ (1 Cor.11:1).

> If anyone wants to argue about this, we have no
> other practice – nor do any of the churches of God
> (1 Cor. 11:16).

> So then, brothers and sisters, stand firm and hold on
> to the traditions you were taught, whether by word
> of mouth or by letter from us (2 Thess. 2:15).

> Brothers and sisters, in the name of our Lord Jesus
> Christ we order you to keep away from every
> believer who is idle and doesn't live according to the
> traditions you received from us. For you yourselves
> know how you ought to follow our example (2
> Thess. 3:6-7a).

These are merely a few of the passages that show how important apostolic patterns and precepts were to Paul and his churches. Little wonder, then, that the earliest Christians had no church buildings, no priests, no youth programs – nothing, in fact, that might have originated in their own minds rather than in the teachings of the apostles. They had no professional "clergy," and the leaders they did have enjoyed a fellowship of leadership as they served together in humility and equality. These early believers had meetings that would amaze us today – highly interactive and participatory, focused on doctrine and teaching, and oozing with *koinonia* (genuine relationships). This stands in obvious contrast to the human-centered operations we call "churches" today.

In our day the commonest fault is for the church to be structured for the sake of man-made traditions rather than for the sake of fidelity to New Testament patterns. This is the emphasis in J. L. Dagg's now classic work, *Manual of Church Order*,[30] first published in 1858. One does not have to agree with everything in the book to appreciate this statement:

---

[30] Harrisonburg, VA: Gano Books, 1990.

[The apostles have] taught us by example how to organize and govern churches. We have no right to reject their instruction and … insist that nothing but positive command shall bind us. Instead of choosing to walk in a way of our own devising, we should take pleasure to walk in the footsteps of those holy men from whom we have received the word of life…. [R]espect for the Spirit by which they were led should induce us to prefer their modes of organization and government to such as our inferior wisdom might suggest.[31]

More recently this idea has been taken up by Steve Atkerson, who directs the *New Testament Restoration Foundation*. Atkerson recommends "a conscious effort to seek to follow the traditions of the Twelve in their church practice. In short, we believe that the patterns for church life evident in the New Testament are not merely *descriptive*, but are actually *prescriptive* (1 Cor. 11:2, 2 Thess. 2:15). Thus, even though we are quite 'traditional' in the New Testament sense, what we advocate is rather nontraditional by contemporary standards."[32] In other words, the New Testament offers a marvelous model of Christian community, even if that model is rarely followed.

In recent years a significant shift in thinking has begun to take place. As an illustration, let me mention a congregation that is located not far from where I live, the Southwest Wake Christian Assembly in Cary, North Carolina. The leadership there decided that the church needed above all else a biblical understanding of its principles and practices. They decided, for example, to forego salaries for their pastoral staff:

We certainly believe there is freedom to have paid staff and biblical examples of the same (1 Tim 5:17-18). We have found that some modern churches

---

[31] *Manual of Church Order*, 84-86.
[32] See http://www.ntrf.org/our-beliefs/index.php.

elevate paid staff (which is not required by Scripture) as a priority over other commands of Scripture (such as caring for the fatherless & widows). Some modern churches tend to rely too heavily on paid staff to provide spiritual food to families rather than expecting men to both lead their families and participate in corporate praise & worship. Therefore we will refrain from paying elders or administrative staff for anything other than reimbursement of legitimate expenses and small stipends until we have firmly established the opposite patterns (caring well for fatherless and widows and men actively participating in corporate praise and worship).[33]

In short, the leaders asked, "Why should we spend the Lord's money on salaries when other needs are more pressing?" They also refuse to spend money on a church building for the same reason.

Your church (and mine) might well ask some similar questions. Has our church grasped the meaning of every-member ministry? Or is it a pyramid with the "clergy" and the "professionals" at the top of the pinnacle and the "lay people" at the bottom? Are parents, and especially fathers, taught that they are the main delivery systems of truth in their homes? Or are they encouraged to abdicate their responsibility to youth group leaders and children's workers? Do we imprison members in programs? Do we ensure that biblical truth is taught and embodied? Do we spend money on buildings that could go instead to missions? A dozen more questions could be asked. Without this emphasis upon and fidelity to apostolic principles and patterns of costly discipleship, the church will never recover or fulfill its mission. The church must organize itself in such a way as to reflect the New Testament's understanding of the Body of Christ. Its structures and practices must reflect those

---

[33] See http://swcassembly.org/principles.

handed down authoritatively by the apostles themselves. There is no secret about how to do it. It just takes time in which to allow the Scriptures to sink into our minds and hearts and so regulate everything we think and do, translating its message into action.

There can no longer be any doubt that our churches have departed from biblical norms. Could it be that we lack the prime essential for discipleship – a personal commitment to the lordship of Christ? I ask myself: Where are the young men and women of today's generation who are determined to stand upon Scripture alone, who are resolved to live by it, and who are committed to obeying it in their lives, their families, and their churches? I venture to say that the twenty-first century church is at a vital crossroads. If we should dare to submit ourselves anew to the full biblical witness to Christ and his church, I believe that the most significant renewal movement in the history of the church may yet await us.

The Radical Reformation: The Anabaptists and Suffering Servanthood

For the Anabaptists the Christian life meant ... discipleship, an obedience to Christ, a separation of the life of the believer from the world in an active pursuit of the priorities of the Kingdom of Christ.

Myron Augsburger[34]

From Anabaptism I have learned that the essential mark of Christian identity is not simply a correct theological evaluation of the person and work of Christ but a conformity to the way of life taught and demonstrated by Jesus in the gospel records. From this has come the capacity to integrate the diverse interests I mentioned earlier: joyful worship with sensitivity to pain; disciplined teaching with openness to the Spirit; and an equal concern for scholarship and spirituality, for community and understanding, for cultural engagement and nonconformity to the world, for evangelism and social action.

Christopher Marshall[35]

---

[34] "Concern for Holiness in the Mennonite Tradition," *The Asbury Seminarian* (Oct. 1980), 28.

New Testament Church Life

I suggested in the previous chapter that the sixteenth century Anabaptists have much to teach us about following Christ.[36] Discipleship – following after Jesus' example – became the key Anabaptist criterion for describing the life of faith. They believed in

- serving instead of ruling
- suffering instead of inflicting suffering
- breaking down walls instead of isolationism
- biblical authority instead of ecclesiastical tradition
- brotherhood instead of hierarchy
- the towel instead of the sword
- the headship of Christ instead of that of any pastor
- the way of peace instead of "just war"
- the church as a living organism instead of as a human institution
- the reign of God instead of a political kingdom
- the catholicity of the true church instead of sectarianism
- the power of suffering instead of the cult of power
  the Bible as a book of the church instead of as a book of scholars

---

[35] "Following Christ Down Under: A New Zealand Perspective on Anabaptism," *Engaging Anabaptism*, ed. John D. Roth (Scottsdale, PA: Herald, 2001), 46.

[36] Some of the writings that have shaped my understanding of the Anabaptist movement include Howard S. Bender, *Conrad Grebel 1498-1526: The Founder of the Swiss Brethren Sometimes Called Anabaptists* (Goshen, IN: Mennonite Historical Society, 1950); ibid., "The Anabaptist Vision," *Mennonite Quarterly Review* 18:2 (April 1944); William R. Estep, *The Anabaptist Story* (Grand Rapids: Eerdmans, 1973); Robert Friedmann, *The Theology of Anabaptism* (Scottsdale, PA: Herald, 1973); E. H. Broadbent, *The Pilgrim Church* (Eugene, OR: Wipf & Stock, 1998); and Leonard Verduin, *The Reformers and Their Stepchildren* (Paris, AR: The Baptist Standard Bearer, 2002).

- loyalty to their heavenly citizenship instead of to the principalities and powers
- Spirit-orientation instead of forced structures of church life
- being a "light to the nations" instead of a Christian enclave
- knowing Christ instead of merely knowing about him
- faith that works (in both senses) instead of dead orthodoxy
- effectual grace as a living reality instead of as a theological dogma
- every-member ministry instead of clergyism
- baptism into Christ instead of baptism into a denomination
- a unity that is lived instead of a unity that is merely extolled
- welcoming the despised and marginalized instead of ignoring them
- a hermeneutic of obedience instead of a hermeneutic of knowledge
- individual conscience instead of theological conformity
- volunteerism instead of professionalism
- allegiance to Christ instead of allegiance to the state

Above all, the Anabaptists believed in obeying Christ's call to abandon self and follow his example of humility, service, and suffering. The way of Jesus, they taught, is the way of suffering servanthood. It is the ultimate in downward mobility.

Recently I met deep underground with a group of persecuted believers in a country I cannot name, men and women who have learned that zeal for the Gospel can lead to hazardous consequences. I taught them that an important aspect of love for Christ is the willingness to risk reputation, property, and life itself. I shared with them what Acts and 1 Thessalonians and

Philippians teach about suffering: that it is the rule, and not the exception, of Christian living. I held up as examples the Anabaptists, whose willingness to lose their lives for others was so profound that the Anabaptist faith has been characterized as a "theology of martyrdom." These Dissenters even offered to take the place of imprisoned brothers.

Anabaptism went beyond the Reformation in adding to Luther's marks of a church (proper preaching and the sacraments) holy living, brotherly love, witnessing, and suffering. For the Anabaptists it was impossible to speak of faith without practicing sacrificial Christian love. According to the Hutterian Peter Walpot, in Protestantism "each looks to his advantage, to his own favor and greed, that he gathers to himself and fills his sack." Contrariwise, the Anabaptists suffered seizure of goods, lengthy imprisonments, even capital punishment. Why? And why should believers today suffer persecution for the cause of Christ? Simply because believers ought at all times to be prepared to share their possessions, their wealth, all they have, however little it may be, to meet the needs of others. And the greatest need of others will always be the Gospel.

Churches today have to make a choice to follow contemporary patterns of ecclesiology or use the early church as a model, as did the Dissenters of the sixteenth century. Although they shared many theological concepts with the Protestant Reformers, the Anabaptists parted company on several crucial points including the separation of church and state (the church must reject all ties with princes and magistrate), believers' baptism (the church consists solely of voluntary members), and restoration rather than reformation (the only valid model of church life is the early church as revealed in the New Testament). Because of these beliefs the Anabaptists endured fierce repression. What sustained them was the reality of Christian community. They truly loved and cared for each other. Like the earliest Christians, they wanted to be known above all by their love, Christian works, and mutual support. Heinrich Bullinger, Zwingli's successor in Zürich, criticized the

Swiss Brethren for teaching that "every Christian is under duty before God to use from motives of love all his possessions to supply the necessities of life to any of his brethren." At the very heart of the dissenting churches was the practice of Christian love and community expressed in material support and concern for outsiders. So genuine and important was the reality of community that the severest penalty was exclusion from the fellowship.

During their gatherings great care was taken that all things were done decently and in order and that all the members had an opportunity to exercise their gifts for the edification of all. Congregations were small enough so that all the members knew each other and could offer any assistance that was necessary. Balthasar Hubmeier wrote in 1526: "For we are not lords of our possessions, but stewards and distributors. There is certainly no one who says that another's goods may be seized and made common; rather, he would gladly give the coat in addition to the shirt." The Anabaptists believed they were required by God to care for their poor members, the ill, widows, and orphans, and that one congregation was to minister to the needs of the other. For example, the toleration enjoyed by the Mennonites in the Netherlands enabled them to use their prosperity to help their persecuted brethren in Switzerland.

Like the Anabaptists of the sixteenth century, who longed for a restoration both in the structures and the practices of the church and whose vision differed from the magisterial model, so I believe it is time for an alternative vision of church and society, one that is Christocentric and follows the pattern of Jesus by obedience to his teaching and his example. More than anything we need a return to the Word of God as the only guide to Christian conduct and thought. To illustrate my point, let me return for a moment to the issue of every-member ministry. Today we find congregational participation in our gatherings squelched by an unbiblical emphasis on the "clergy" and a corresponding passivity among the "laypeople." The motivation behind limiting congregational participation is undoubtedly noble (to ensure "quality," to protect against heresies, to maintain order, etc.). Still, such motivations are biblically unsustainable. For example, quality can be just as low in a church that practices monological preaching as in one that encourages mutual participation. Besides, the worst heresies in the Christian church have not been promulgated by laypeople but rather by professionally trained theologians. Finally, as we saw in chapter 2, only a form of corporate ministry in which all believers are free to exercise their gifts and share their insights comports with the New Testament. Along with Romans 12, Ephesians 4, and 1 Peter 4, 1 Corinthians 14 teaches that the church is a Body comprised of many members, each of whom has something important to contribute to the whole. Apparently Paul believed that God may speak or act through any member of the church for the benefit of the entire community. The result must have been a richness and diversity scarcely known today in many of our churches.

I am not saying that every member ministry entails either the participation of all believers in every gathering or the abolishing of leadership. Rather, it involves a wide participation by those who are Spirit-led. A communal approach to ministry would seem, then, to be a core value of the church and should be encouraged by the leadership, whose role is more facilitative than dominant. Common dangers must be recognized and avoided (e.g., over-participation by some, fear of being criticized by the group, passivity). When it is felt that the conventional monologue is appropriate, it will be helpful to stop for questions and interaction with one's hearers, if not in the middle then at least at the end. Jesus' own teaching was frequently characterized by verbal interaction, while the apostle Paul clearly engaged in dialogue with his Christian audiences. Even the famous Christian orator Chrysostom interrupted his discourses frequently to ask questions in order to make sure he was understood. Every believer is a priest, and although congregations certainly benefit from the theological expertise of some, the New Testament knows no cult of the expert who ignores the gifts of the people.

The Anabaptists and Clerical Ministry

In speaking of the doctrine of the priesthood of all believers, some readers may be thinking I am denying the need for leaders (elders/deacons) in a New Testament church. Nothing could be further from the truth. But before we can consider the role of congregational leadership we must begin with a fundamental reality – the fact that in the New Testament church there are no priests. And there are no priests precisely because Jesus himself is the one and only mediator between God and humans. It was not until the advent of Christendom that people were needed who could serve as mediators. Simple believers could no longer approach this God of sacerdotal Christianity. As in the Old Testament economy, holy persons were now required who would themselves be able to offer holy sacrifices in holy places (now called "sanctuaries"). In the New Testament, the people (*laos*) themselves were the bearers of the sacred. Jesus had radically abolished the clergy-laity distinction of Judaism.

It seems to me that we must root out from our minds any acceptance of such a sacral view of the church. When I say that Jesus is against sacralism, I am not saying that he is against ministries such as preaching and teaching and leading. It was he, in fact, who gifted the church with the equipping ministry of shepherd-teacher (Eph. 4:11). The trouble is that there is very little in the New Testament that would support the thesis that the church is to have a special class of Christians who rule over the church in the place of the Head. The best example of this faulty notion is found in Hebrews 13:17, where the expression "those who rule over you" is quite possibly a gross mistranslation of the Greek. The linguistic arguments I have come across in support of an "office" of elder (in terms of title and status, not function) are weak. I earnestly believe that the clerical interpretation of such passages as Hebrews 13:17, although advocated by honest exegetes, is a falsification. How is it that when the apostle Paul addresses problems in a local church (say Corinth or Colosse) he never calls upon the "clergy"

to resolve the issues? If one supposes that the clergy were to
rule the church and handle all serious problems, this fact is
inexplicable. We can go a step further. In 1 Thessalonians. 5:14
Paul specifically requests the "brothers" – not the church leaders
– to admonish those believers who were unruly. And why, if the
believers were to defer to their leaders in the case of church
discipline, did Paul command the church to expel the
unrepentant sinner in 1 Corinthians 5:4-5? We have no right to
go beyond the clear pattern of the New Testament and insist
upon a clergy-laity distinction. It is clear that the New Testament
elder was not a proud, prestigious, and powerful ruler but rather
a humble, gentle, and deeply spiritual "brother" (see Matt. 23:8)
who in the spirit of Jesus was called to serve rather than be
served (Mark 10:45).

To the Anabaptists, then, a clerical ministry seemed out of
step with both the spirit and the letter of the New Testament.
As Hebrews 13:7 shows, the authority of leaders was based not
on their position or title but rather on their example (*anastrophe*)
and faithfulness (*pistis*). The relationship of members to leaders
was not one of duty but of love and respect. We have to
recognize that theologians themselves have done much to create
this confusion. Jesus' model of church leadership has nothing to
do with status or office. This monumental misunderstanding of
the New Testament seems to me to be one of the flagrant
proofs that the Anabaptists' return to the doctrine of the
priesthood of all believers was both necessary and inevitable for
a group so earnestly seeking the truth of the Word of God.[37] I
see this same truth-seeking spirit at work today when I see
younger leaders eschewing grand titles such as "reverend" or

---

[37] An early Brethren tract complained about the monopoly of the
preacher and the failure of the state churches to obey Paul's
instructions in 1 Corinthians 14 that every member should contribute
something to the Body when the church met together. See Paul
Preachey, "Answer of Some Who are Called (Ana)baptists Why They
Do not Attend the Churches: A Swiss Brethren Tract," *Mennonite
Quarterly Review* 45 (Jan. 1971), 5-32.

"minister" or "senior pastor," preferring instead to be called "brother" or simply by their first names. This kind of thinking is contrary to every man-made system or philosophy. A Christianity that seeks no power, no prestige, no position but instead prefers humiliation, service, even suffering? Unthinkable – except, perhaps, to someone committed to the Jesus paradigm.

Many scholars have noted the rapidity with which the practice of the early church about mutual ministry was abandoned in favor of a clericalized, professionalized, and institutionalized Christianity. In the early Anabaptist community individualism gave way to the principles of cooperation, mutual dependency, and the common celebration of Christ's achievements. It was understood that for the Body of Christ to function as its Head intended, its many otherwise diverse parts had to act as a single entity. There had to be a recognition that each part was important, and in fact the apparently weakest parts of the Body were the indispensable ones. The Anabaptists took Jesus seriously when he said that in the kingdom of God the weakest and lowliest members of the community were to be given priority. They believed that Christians should be committed to voluntary forms of organization in which there is no place for hierarchy or coercive structures. However, once Christianity became fashionable, the goal became power, or status, or numbers, or wealth, or size, or large gatherings – all tokens of secular politics. I tried to say something of this in *Paul, Apostle of Weakness.*[38] Are we to think that God cannot work through the weak? That is the *only* way he works. But the advent of Christendom does not change at all what God has accomplished through history. Jesus Christ, the Son, humbled himself and in so doing subverted culture: human power structures are now radically broken.

---

[38] New York: Lang, 1984.

A New Covenant Approach

Thus far we have argued that the greatest threat to Christianity is Christendom. Christendom is an effort of the human race to abolish true Christianity. It does not attempt to do this overtly but under the pretext that it is genuine Christianity. Here again, popular beliefs of theologians and biblical scholars have perpetuated the false idea that Christendom is acceptable to God. In this whole arena of thought there is a grievous lack of any exegetical precision. At the same time, the sixteenth century Anabaptists, led not by Protestant or Reformed thought but by the Scriptures themselves, radically challenged the entrenchment of Christendom in European culture. A major difference between the Anabaptists and the Protestants was their view that the Scriptures provided models both for theology as well as for church organization. The Anabaptists were interested in *restitutio*, not *reformatio*. They considered themselves neither Protestant nor Catholic but a third way. The Bible, not tradition, provided the patterns for church organization just as plainly as it revealed the basic theological content of the faith.

The Reformers were unwilling to make such a radical break with the past. The churches remained established and the parish system was maintained. By contrast, the Anabaptists understood the example of early Christianity to be a binding norm for Christians of all ages. A classic example was infant baptism. The Anabaptists argued that since the rite could not be found in the New Testament, it could not be used in a movement trying to emulate the life of the early church. To them the rite was non-apostolic and therefore an insidious shame to genuine Christianity. Again, the life of Jesus was central in Anabaptist thought. Since Jesus was fully grown when he received baptism, the rite must be an adult matter. However – and this is a vital point – the real issue in baptism was not simply a return to the New Testament pattern. Rather, it involved a promise to walk in newness of life, that is, to live according to the Word of God by refusing to let sin reign in the mortal body. In other words, the local church, entry into which was through baptism, was to be a community of *saints*. The Anabaptists argued that without such concern for morality and genuine repentance, a slipshod practice of spiritual laxity would inevitably result.

It is clear, then, that the Anabaptists were more interested in the New Testament than the Old. It was only the New Testament that contained the explicit teaching of Christ and his apostles. The Old Testament was not rejected, of course. It was simply subjected to the doctrines found in the Gospels and the Epistles. According to Pilgram Marpeck, the Old Testament must be distinguished from the New Testament as the foundation must be distinguished from the house. John Kiwiet summarizes Marpeck's hermeneutics as follows:

> Der alte Bund war eine Zeit des Suchens und des Dürstens und erst der Neue Bund eine Zeit des Findens und Stillens. Die Verheissung an die Alten geht im Neuen Bund in Erfülling [sic]. Die Finsternis wird zu Licht und der Tod zu Leben. Es ist wie der Unterschied zwischen gestern und heute; das Alte ist vorbeigegangen, und das Neue ist gekommon.[39]

> The Old Covenant was a time of seeking and thirsting and the New Covenant a time of finding and stillness. The promise to the ancients finds its fulfillment in the New Covenant. Darkness turns to light and death to life. It is like the difference between yesterday and today; the old has gone away, and the new has arrived.

Marpeck's point is that revelation was progressive and partial before Christ. He felt that the Reformers had mistaken the foundation of the house for the house itself. Marpeck's two-

---

[39] John Kiwiet, *Pilgram Marpeck* (Kassel: Oncken, 1958), 101-102.

covenant theology was based on Paul's letter to the Galatians and the Epistle to the Hebrews, which taught that the highest court of appeal for all teaching concerning the church was the New Covenant. In short, the Scriptures must be interpreted *Christologically*.

This is one reason the Anabaptists looked with disfavor on professional pastors whose support came through tithes in the parish system. Unlike Old Testament Israel, their leaders were laymen, since Christ's offering as High Priest was deemed to be exclusive. Their pastors, moreover, were chosen by the entire congregation according to the pattern established in the New Testament (Acts 14:23; 20:17, 28). They were supported by voluntary offerings (though many indeed supported themselves). In addition, age-integrated ministry was to be practiced because this was the clear pattern of the New Testament. God has revealed himself to his people regardless of mental capacity (Matt. 11:25) and has given his Spirit to all, regardless of age, sex, or standing in society (Acts 2:17-18). Jesus himself taught all ages together, a classic example being the feeding of 5,000 men, "besides women and children" (Matt. 14:21). He often used children as examples of discipleship. As a young man, Jesus himself sat "among the teachers, listening to them and asking them questions" (Luke 2:47). The church was therefore to be a believers' church. Free churchmen placed the apostrophe after the "s" in "believers" to emphasize the communal and corporate quality of belief, in contrast to individualism.

As for the place of meeting, lavish sanctuaries were no longer necessary since Christ had abolished the Old Testament priesthood. John Darby, one of the founders of the Brethren church, encouraged the construction of simple chapels or assemblies with architecture that emphasized the priesthood of all believers. Pulpits and platforms were avoided. A typical chapel was a square room with a table and chairs for the speakers. Darby insisted on sitting among the members during the service and standing among them when he spoke (rather than from behind the table). The Anabaptists denied the significance of church buildings since physical structures were irrelevant to God. The buildings themselves were emblems of mere formalism. Large stone structures could never replace the true church of Christ that is comprised of two or three living stones gathered in his Spirit. They felt that with the addition of large numbers of extravagant temples the church had compromised with worldly standards of success. The Anabaptists energetically condemned this "externalization" of the Body of Christ.

Moreover, in Anabaptism appeal was made to the plain man's judgment, unspoiled by the university. Those who toiled with their hands (craftsmen) or who worked in the soil (peasants) were presumed to be more receptive and teachable than those who had been corrupted by the folly of worldly wisdom. Here a certain irony arises, of course, for among the radical thinkers of Anabaptism there were not a few university trained men whose knowledge of the Scriptures and of the original languages of the Bible were unsurpassed. I cannot refrain here from referring to my fellow Basler Conrad Grebel, who studied at the Grossmünster in Zürich for six years before becoming one of the 81 students to register at the University of Basel in the winter semester of 1514. At Basel he lived in the bursa (college) that was under the direction of the city's leading humanist scholar, Heinrich Loriti (Glarean). From Basel he traveled to Vienna to continue his studies, and from there to Paris. Perhaps the Anabaptists' attitude toward scholarship was based to a degree upon their work ethic. Hard work was considered a virtue. The peasant who worked with his own hands in cooperation with God's nature was thought to have keener insight than the scribe with his multitude of books. So the Anabaptists might argue: "How can those who know the Master miss his simple and straightforward words in Matthew 23 condemning the use of honorific titles?" To the Anabaptists, use of such titles seemed the very culmination of worldliness and power. Their message was simple: *Let the Reformers cling to the old ideas of Christendom. We will seek a thoroughgoing restitution of the church as it had been before the rise of* Constantine.

It's interesting to note that William Tyndale considered the chief cause of all the trouble in the church of his day to be the fact that the Scriptures of God were hidden from the people's eyes. So he gave the world its first English New Testament translated directly from the original Greek. We may ask why such an act deserved the implacable hatred of the church hierarchy. Tyndale was deemed a heretic because he challenged the established ideas of his day. He translated the Greek word *presbuteros* as "elder" instead of "priest," the word *ekklesia* as "congregation" instead of "church," and the word *metanoia* as "repentance" instead of "penance." The Roman Church, built on penance and holy orders, could not tolerate such a "blasphemer" and "heretic." In a similar way, the sixteenth century Anabaptists challenged the Catholic, Lutheran, and Reformed establishments. Centuries later Barth and Brunner would question the church-state system from within. Why, then, should it surprise us today when Christians engage in responsible criticism of their own denominations? The goal of the Anabaptists, as has often been said, was to cut the tree back to the root and thus free the church of the suffocating growth of ecclesiastical tradition. That this goal is being revived in our day should be the cause of great rejoicing.

Apolitical Christianity

In order to understand what Anabaptist theology means for us today, we must also look at their attitude toward the state. Allow me to begin the discussion with a brief personal anecdote. I had just arrived as a doctoral student in Basel when I happened upon a sporting goods store that had a large display window facing the street. To my amazement I saw something I never dreamed I would see in landlocked Switzerland – a surfboard with the word "Kailua" on it, a reference to the beach where I grew up in Hawaii. I was delightfully surprised by this discovery.

Warm, happy memories of my hometown and its magnificent beach came to me. I had discovered in that shop window the sense of belonging that I had lost in that far-away city on the Rhine.

This simple incident contained an important lesson for me: the power of symbols, identity, belonging, security. That is what culture is all about. I mention this because it seems to me that the Anabaptists of the sixteenth century were willing to do what few of their religious counterparts today are willing to do: abandon "security" and live as true pilgrims and strangers on earth. The Anabaptists did just that, and they did it in the face of terrible persecution from their contemporaries, Catholics and Protestants alike, who contemptuously labeled them "Re-Baptizers." In sixteenth century Europe a person could not be called a dirtier name. The Anabaptists were considered the arch-enemies of Europe's entrenched religious and political institutions. They were regarded as more than ill-informed and antisocial. In a world of religious wars and economic rape, they were deemed to be demonically-inspired heretics. When the nation-states demanded them to bless their ambitions and sanctify their warring, the Anabaptists simply refused. But they weren't anarchists. Their view of a just and limited state was self-consciously Bible-based, and by withdrawing from the "culture" of their day they struck a radical blow for liberty and conscience, a blow still felt to this day.

Today the nation-state has become the most murderous and destructive force the world has ever known. Not just the horrific actions of totalitarian governments but the unlawful actions of legitimate governments cry out for redress. The church has become so domesticated, so "acculturated," that it willingly tolerates the straightjacket of authoritarian theologies. It has forgotten the words of Jesus that his kingdom is not of this world, that his followers do not have to fight to advance his cause, and that his kingly authority comes from elsewhere. The Anabaptists faced an important question that still faces churches today: how to follow Jesus and do that responsibly in the political sphere. It was in direct consequence of their understanding of Christian discipleship that they became apolitical. Their refusal to take part in the magistery or to take an oath or to participate in violence was founded on their conception of two opposing kingdoms, one characterized by peace, the other by strife. While submitting to the authorities for conscience' sake, they refused to allow the state any right to make decisions in the church, rejected the absolutist claims of the state, and refused to participate in religious warfare. Their pacifism had a profound theological orientation, and it was precisely for this reason they were persecuted so ruthlessly by the established churches.

Their views represent a theology of the state we can neither hear nor accept today. The Beatitudes have become absurd and unacceptable. We sterilize the words of Christ or reserve them for obscurantists. To declare that Christ's kingdom is not of this world, that the state is both corruptible and corrupting, that the paternal power of government inevitably leads to servitude – such ideas are condemned as the notions of self-deceived revolutionaries. The persistence of this sacral mentality helps to explain certain American traits that foreigners find so baffling: the sacrosanct attitude toward statists such as Ann Coulter, Sean Hannity, and Rush Limbaugh; the biblical metaphors employed by American politicians to justify the spread of democracy by force; and the rancor against critics of the state such as Ron Paul, Lew Rockwell, and Chuck Baldwin – to name just three.

In 1967 Michael Novak wrote, "It is very difficult for many American Christians even to conceive the possibility that American civilization is profoundly anti-Christian, *precisely in those very places where it is most pious, patriotic, and full of noble sentiment.*"[40] Novak is right. We attack the "issues" of the day and drag in Scriptures to support this stand or that. We become so preoccupied with politics that we forget to preach and live the Gospel. We talk "peace" when there is none. Never has America

---

[40] "We Need a New Reformation...HERE!" (*Together* 11, Oct. 1967) .

sought so diligently to make itself safe as now and never with poorer results. We have resigned ourselves to unholy alliances with politicians with the excuse that "nobody is perfect." False saviors offer their fads and panaceas and Christians join them with glee. Certainly American evangelicals have no right to point a condemning finger at the established churches of Europe.

And what of the Anabaptists? They taught that the church is not only apolitical but antipolitical in the sense that it regards political power as inevitably idolatrous. The church is to seek the kingdom of *heaven* and *its* righteousness. It therefore refuses to confer any value on political power but instead radically questions it. With Constantine's victory at the Milvian Bridge, however, the church became invested with political power, and it has sought political power ever since. It acquiesced where Jesus resisted: the church accepts all the kingdoms of the earth from Satan. It forges an alliance with the state, which it now seeks to Christianize. Christianity becomes the state religion, and the combination of truth and political power leads to the abuses we know so well today: blind support of the state and its policies; spreading the Gospel by force; refusing to challenge state propaganda; failing to question the truth and validity of the alliance of church and empire; redefining patriotism as nationalism; attaching the label "Christian" to political parties; justifying revolution in the name of "justice" (never defined); and using political power to secure to itself advantages. All of this is an absurd contradiction to the life and teaching of Jesus, who had nothing whatsoever to do with politics. To him such things were of no interest or importance. He neither entered political debates nor encouraged them. He supported neither the followers of Rome nor their enemies. And the earliest Christian community was of the same mind.

This is a lesson the evangelical church needs to learn today. Randall Balmer is right when he says that "the lessons of American history and the example of mainline Protestantism teach us that religious fervor and conviction function best on the margins of society and not in the councils of power and influence."[41] Today we have a church of the right and a church of the left, a church for Republicans and a church for Democrats, a church for gay marriage and a church against it, and on and on it goes. Adulteration by political power has many faces indeed. Christianity in America is now seen as an indispensable tool for political campaigning (the exact opposite of what it is scripturally), and its biblical language and metaphors are used to support our wars of conquest. Satan must be jumping with joy. He would have the church conform to the age. He would have us forget that we are pilgrims and strangers, alien citizens of heaven. He would have us compromise and cut a deal to get the kingdoms of the earth by a shortcut. But Jesus shows us that we do not have to bow to the devil to win the world.

Regardless of what one thinks of Anabaptism, all true Christians must be for peace. This does not necessarily mean that we must all be pacifists. But even if one believes that violence may become necessary in emergencies, we are all to be peacemakers. The Gospel is a Gospel of peace. God is the God of peace. As followers of Christ we must think about peace, talk about peace, pray for peace, and work for peace. Politics inevitably seeks to use religion for narrow political purposes. The church, however, should be an entity that transcends all earthly loyalties and that constantly calls the power of the state into question. This is what the Anabaptists of the sixteenth century believed and taught, and, I think, it is worth believing and teaching in the twenty-first.

Vaclav Havel once said that people living in Western democracies are just as manipulated as people living in totalitarian regimes, albeit in more subtle ways. Isn't this true of politics? In the end, I believe the most effective contribution the church can make to politics is its faithful, even stubborn, adherence to a strict separationist stand, with primary concern to guard the wall that divides church and state.

---

[41] *Thy Kingdom Come*, 32.

The Brotherhood of All Believers

Two other aspects of Anabaptist thought merit our consideration: their self-identification as a brotherhood, and their commitment to missions. If we were to read Matthew 23 and take Jesus' words at face value, we would come away with the notion that he was not very impressed with all the titles we make so much of today. We would feel that all this talk about "doctor" and "reverend" and "senior pastor" is somewhat superficial, that titles are merely manmade epithets and quite contrary to the idea of a brotherhood church. At the same time, if we were to read the New Testament epistles we would get a pretty clear hint of what Christian leadership looked like. It is a very far cry from the world's model of a CEO or institutional president. And there is to be no pride, no bossiness, no "swagger" whatsoever. The New Testament is always insisting on mutuality and on stressing the fact that we are all brothers (or sisters) in Christ, though, of course, some are "big brothers" in the sense that they have more wisdom and experience than others. We must remind ourselves that in the passage where Jesus forbids the use of honorific titles he gives us a reason: "… for only one is your Teacher, and you are all brothers" (Matt. 23:8). Jesus commands us to foreswear such titles, not because they are evil in and of themselves, but because they maximize what should be minimized in the family of God, where each member has equal value and worth.

When Jesus says, "Do not be called Rabbi" (Matt. 23:8), he means (so I take the Greek), "Do not make people call you Rabbi." All of this would have been quite acceptable to the Anabaptists. For them, the essence of Christianity was discipleship. All else was subordinated to that. And what is a disciple? A disciple is one who follows Christ (*Nachfolge Christi*) and not any man, no matter how important or eminent or exalted that man may be in the world's eyes, or in the church's. Discipleship for the Anabaptists refers not simply to a life that is spiritually motivated but one that is externally patterned after

Christ's own person and work. The Anabaptists assumed that the life and teaching of Jesus were to be replicated both in principle and in form by his followers. The Lord's rejection of social strictures, his freedom from cultural entanglements, his humility and lowliness of mind – all these were accepted as normal for all true disciples.

Such beliefs contradicted, of course, the fundamental convictions of more than a thousand years of ecclesiastical history. The Anabaptist faith was a radical departure from that history not least because it clashed with culturally entrenched traditions of the Reformation such as the clergy-laity division. The Anabaptists were content to call each other "brethren," in keeping with Jesus' teaching. It seems to me, therefore, that if we are to be true to the Scriptures we must abandon the idea that there is any positive value in referring to each other by manmade titles instead of by the term of endearment enjoined upon us by our Lord. I do not want people to call me "Doctor Black" because they think I prefer the title or place any weight on academic credentials per se. I don't. If people choose to use the title "doctor" because they cannot break with tradition or because they cannot conceive of me as their brother, I understand. But my preference is to be called "brother Dave" or "brother Black" (if you feel you must use the last name) or simply "Dave." Please don't think that this is a mark of modesty on my part. I actually believe, am completely persuaded in fact, that the term "brother" (or "sister") is the highest, most honorable, most glorious title that a follower of Jesus can be given by a fellow Christian (see Heb. 2:11-12). It marks the relationship we will all enjoy in eternity when every earthly title will disappear for good.[42]

---

[42] This point is made in several places by Donald Kraybill in *The Upside-Down Kingdom* (Scottsdale, PA: Herald, 2003): "Tagging each other with titles has no place in the upside-down kingdom where everyone stands on equal ground" (226). "Kingdom people will also strive to minimize hierarchy in social governance" (238). "Titles are foreign to the body of Christ. Terms like Doctor and Reverend

In his poem "Adler und Taube," Goethe describes a wounded eagle that was forced to spend some time in the valley among the lowly pigeons. The joyful and active pigeons were surprised at the unhappy eagle in the beautiful surroundings of the valley. Looking up at the snowcapped mountains the eagle knew that if he attempted to tell them about his world, they would not understand. And yet, writes Goethe, no matter how great the difference between the mountains and the meadows, both the eagle and the pigeon are parts of one world. So the brightest theologian and the newest convert are members of the same Body of Christ. If you are a pastor and decide you must have a title, might I recommend "servant pastor" instead of "senior pastor"? If I'm not mistaken, the congregation will be pleasantly surprised by that language. After all, as a leader you are called to be the lowest servant of all, aren't you?

The Anabaptists and Missions

Finally, I want to speak briefly about what Christians call missions. (The term does not appear in the Greek New Testament.) Unlike many Christians today, and unlike perhaps the majority of Reformers of the sixteenth century, the Anabaptists believed that the Great Commission was the responsibility of every believer and could not be left to pastors or mission agencies. An old Anabaptist hymn puts it this way:

> *As God his Son was sending*
> *Into this world of sin,*
> *His Son is now commending*
> *That we this world should win.*
> *He sends us and commissions*
> *To preach the gospel clear,*
> *To call upon all nations*
> *To listen and to hear.*

---

perpetuate status differences unbefitting the spirit of Christ" (239). "We call each other by our first name, for we have one Master and one Lord, Jesus Christ" (256).

Anabaptist scholar Alan Kreider has described in several of his writings the phenomenal growth that took place in the church of the first three centuries.[43] He has observed that the church grew rapidly not because of training programs in evangelism or admonitions to "share one's faith." Precisely the opposite was true. The pre-Constantine church grew by leaps and by bounds, says Kreider, *because it had a new way of living*. The same was true of the Anabaptist movement. It grew by "fascination" as well as by words, by its Jesus-likeness. A core commitment of the Anabaptists – and by "core" I mean just that – was to implement the missionary mandate entrusted to the church by Christ. And this mandate was not just the prerogative of selected professionals but the privilege and responsibility of the simplest believer.

In speaking of the missionary heart of the Anabaptists my highest hope is that it might help us to implement biblical principles in our own lives and fellowships. I believe that if we are open to a fresh leading of the Holy Spirit, at whatever cost to our present way of living, we cannot help but become more missional in the way we think and act. The purpose of the Anabaptist movement was more than to recall Christians to their biblical roots. At every point the Anabaptists sought to correct the notion of their contemporaries that the Great Commission had been fulfilled by Christ's original apostles. It was this emphasis that explains the contempt, and even disgust, that some of the magisterial Reformers felt for the missionary program of the Dissenters.

Our own situation is much like that of the Anabaptists. Today we have to strip off the false notion that missions is only for professionals. Jesus is asking his followers today to take seriously not just the gathering but the going forth. What we must learn to say to the world is: "Here we are. We are willing to make any sacrifice to see that you know Jesus. We are not asking you to

---

[43] See, e.g., *The Origins of Christendom in the West* (London: T & T Clark, 2001); *A Way of Living for God's Nation* (Eugene, OR: Wipf & Stock, 2008).

come to church with us. We love you right where you are. We love you no matter what you do to us. If we have to build a hut next to you for the rest of time just to witness to the love and grace of the Lord Jesus, we are going to make that effort. We're not going to take you out of your environment or make you a part of an institution just to keep the institution going."

For the Anabaptists, the church was a community consisting of those who had a vital relationship with Jesus as Lord and Savior. It was the brotherhood of the redeemed, purchased by Christ's spilled blood. It was the fellowship of the regenerated who as "living stones" were being built up into a holy temple. It was the body of Christ-centered sharing where each bore the other's burdens and thus fulfilled the law of Christ. The church was all of this to the Anabaptists. *But it was much more than this.* The church was the community of those who not only worshiped God and learned of Christ but who witnessed and served, proclaiming in word and deed the Lord Jesus Christ and his salvation to anyone who would listen. For the Anabaptists the biblical church was a *Great Commission church* – witnessing, evangelizing, and ministering in love both to each other and to the outside world. For them the whole of life was to be one of service and sacrifice. Members of free churches were not to be left alone to their own devices. This meant that they would not only serve the needs of the brethren but carry their witness into the world. No words of Jesus meant more to the Anabaptists than the Great Commission. They believed that the true church was obliged to take that commission seriously. We are obliged, I think, to do no less today.

Conclusion: Why Study the Anabaptists?

A question may legitimately be asked by those who have had the patience to complete the reading of the preceding pages: Why should a 21st century Christian so vigorously promote Anabaptist ideals? The answer is that Anabaptist principles can be applied to many modern problems of church life – restoring church discipline to our nominal memberships, fostering the ministry of the "laity," promoting global missions – to name but a few.

I didn't write this chapter because I'm in favor of belittling the work of the Magisterial Reformers. For clarity's sake I must repeat that I am indicting the Reformers only because they were inconsistent with their own principles of reformation. Here, of course, I am not alone in my thinking. As far back as 1914, Henry Vedder, in his book *The Reformation in Germany*, had this to say about the Anabaptists:

> They were the only party among those protesting against the errors of Rome who were logical and thoroughgoing. They alone accepted in absolute faith and followed to its necessary consequences the principle avowed by the leading reformers, that the Scriptures were the sole source of religious authority.... The Anabaptists alone had penetrated beneath the surface of traditional Christianity and comprehended the real Gospels of Jesus.... In a word, the Anabaptists were the real reformers, and the only real reformers, of the Sixteenth century.[44]

I hope no reader will suppose that Anabaptism is being put forward as an alternative to the Word of God, as if any man-made movement is preferable to the testimony of inspired Scripture. The record of Anabaptism is by no means a spotless one. Like every movement of the Holy Spirit it is the story of a weak, stammering church that moved over a field of ecclesiastical rubble. I'm not condoning everything in the movement or offering pious panaceas.[45] If I have left an overly

---

[44] Henry C. Vedder, *The Reformation in Germany* (New York: Macmillan, 1914), 345.
[45] I agree with Howard Snyder's perspective, *The Problem of Wineskins* (Downers Grove: InterVarsity, 1975), 196-97: "There are several points of contact between the approach advocated in this book and the thinking of such groups as the Anabaptists, Quakers, and Plymouth

positive impression, it is because I believe that an appreciation
of Anabaptism can prove fruitful in many areas of Christian life
and witness. The important point is this: Anabaptism was a valid,
if incomplete, representation of Christ's Body – nothing more,
nothing less. I also hope that this chapter might have a
mollifying effect on those modern-day traditionalists who view
dissent as inherently misguided and dissenters as mere fanatics
or *Schwärmer*. (The parallel with Luther and Zwingli will not
escape the reader.)

I suspect that church institutions as they are now known are
incapable of thoroughgoing renewal. It is my view that new
church plants are the most likely bodies to reflect early
Christianity rather than the proud establishments of
Christendom. I would like to think that at least the weekly
observance of the breaking of the bread and the ministry of all
believers could be restored to church practice, if not also a
stronger congregational discipline (done in love, of course). I
think that everyone would agree with me if I said that Luther
and Zwingli were not averse to using the state as an instrument
to achieve their own purposes. In the Anabaptist perspective, the
leaders of the Reformation were no less tyrants than
Constantine because they also enforced religious conformity by
civil power. The pomp and display, the ambition and the pride
of Christendom, seen in both their Roman Catholic and
Protestant forms, were the precise opposite of the submissive
humility that characterized Anabaptism. One does not have to

Brethren. I hold that these groups took much of their dynamic from
their rediscovery of basic biblical truths about the church, even while
they mixed these with others which were less biblical. Because of the
historically conditioned nature of each of these groups – the "cultural
factor" – no one of them (or even the early church for that matter)
may be taken as a perfect model for the church today. This is not what
I propose in this book, nor is this book merely a restatement of the
views of earlier reform movements. Rather it is a call for serious
reflection on the problem of church structure and for a fresh
application of basic biblical concepts of the church to our age."

be a biblical scholar to recognize the parallels that exist with today's American form of God-and-Country evangelicalism. Just as Martin Niemöller unflinchingly told crowds in Nazi Germany to follow the "Jewish rabbi, Jesus Christ," so those who are called to follow Christ in the midst of a statist church will need tremendous courage. If there is perhaps a side benefit of the current imbroglio in Iraq, it is that it is providing the crucible and training ground for a new generation of Christian thinkers who are willing to question the status quo vis-à-vis church-state relationships.

This is one reason why I can't agree with those who say that Anabaptism represented a "wing" of the Reformation. If it was a wing, it was one that the bird tried desperately to sever from its body. Excluding fanatical groups such as the Münsterites and the Antitrinitarians, the mainstream Anabaptists rejected out of hand the organizational form of the state-church system. Membership in the Body of Christ was based solely on a voluntary confession of faith in Jesus and a commitment to walk in Christian discipleship according to the pacific and brotherly teachings of Christ. No one was automatically a Christian by virtue of being born and baptized in a particular geographical region. Anabaptism was reserved for those who confessed Christ. The church of today deserves scathing criticism for its lack of discernment in this area and its easy-believism. The essence of Christianity, so the Anabaptists taught, was obedience to Christ. High ethical standards were set and maintained by church discipline. Selfless sharing was emphasized, though not to the point that a person would give so much that he or she would also need to be cared for. The Hutterites believed that individualism was a sin against God. Contrast our churches today and the way we pay lip-service to Body Life, mutual participation, and every-member ministry. I do not know a way of describing this abysmal state of affairs other than as an unhealthy dependence on professional ministers. There is very little fleshing out of the doctrine of the priesthood of all believers except on certain "special days" such as Youth Sunday or Men's Day.

However, I think even the severest critics of Anabaptism would agree on one thing. The Anabaptists practiced what they preached. They were truly a family. Decision-making was based on consensus, not popular vote. Issues were discussed until the brethren agreed and could say, "It seemed good to the Holy Spirit and to us." (What a far cry from our enslavement to Robert's Rules of Order!) They developed a true mutuality and sense of brotherhood. The Lord's Supper, practiced weekly, was as vital to the maintenance of this fellowship as baptism was to its beginning. The Supper was a memorial of the Lord's suffering and death and a symbol of his presence, not in the bread and the cup but in the fellowship of the faithful. Membership in this fellowship called for an obedient walk in Christian discipleship according to the teachings of Jesus, seen not least in a commitment to implement the missionary mandate entrusted by the Lord to his apostles. This commission was binding on the church and thus the responsibility of every baptized believer. Above all, the Anabaptists taught that the church must follow the guidelines of the New Testament as to its confession of faith and its organizational patterns. For them the Bible was as ambiguous as to the doctrine of the church as it was to the doctrine of salvation. Their ecclesiology called for non-conformity to the world, the separation of church and state, and serving others in meekness in the spirit of Christ. The church is neither Catholic nor Protestant but simply Christian, they argued. Christ the King is the only Head of the church. An authoritative ministry by the elders was therefore out of keeping with the spirit as well as the letter of the New Testament.

And so we are left to ponder a question: will anything in our churches change? The very fact that the strongest arguments, the most rigorous exegesis, the most time-tested values are of no avail is proof that we are faced with a conscious decision made in the light of thorough knowledge. *Obedience, not knowledge, is our problem.* The church in America has reached a Rubicon, and it will either cross it or it won't. Even though a good many thinking people regard the "system" as fatally flawed, as utterly frightful, they feel caught by an inescapable dilemma. They reject Christendom in principle, but a renewal is no longer desirable, at least in the current state of the church. Whether we call ourselves conventional, emergent, or convergent, the church is rushing nowhere at an incredible rate of speed. We know the dangers of our faddish programs but we go on building them anyway.

It is not my intention to argue that the church is beyond renewal. I love the church. Why else would I have chosen to teach servant-leaders if I didn't? I have simply tried to remind myself (and anyone who will join me in thinking through the issues) that the way forward is backward – back to the sixteenth century, and back even further to the radicals of the first century, the original generation of Christians that turned the world right side up. I believe that the old values are still worth pursuing. And – thank God! – they have not been completely forgotten. They continue to speak to believers today, hearkening back to a time when the church was Spirit-led, simple, and solidly evangelistic. If the church of today decides it knows better than the New Testament how to conduct itself, then so be it. The fact is that the modern church has sought greatness and attained power instead. And therein lies its ultimate tragedy.

When the centaur Nessus was fatally wounded by Heracles, he persuaded Heracles' wife Deianira to keep a saucer of his blood as a charm to preserve her husband's love. Later on Deianira dipped one of Heracles' robes into the blood, thinking thereby to keep him faithful to her. The robe, however, stuck to Heracles' skin, and to remove it he had to tear away large pieces of his flesh. What can free us from the Nessus' robe we have woven for ourselves? It is certainly not Anabaptism or any other movement in church history. Of that I am certain. Freedom from our bondage can only be accomplished by the moving of God, an interplay of forces and mechanisms that is completely beyond our control.

The Priestly Kingdom: Communal Ecclesiology and Every-Member Ministry

The church is never a place, but always a people; never a fold but always a flock; never a sacred building but always a believing assembly. The church is you who pray, not where you pray. A structure of brick or marble can no more be a church than your clothes of serge or satin can be you.

John F. Havlik[46]

The FDR-ing of the Church

Americans have always been a hard-working, resilient people. That is, until FDR. Today, as a result of government social programs, we have come to depend more and more on the federal government to take care of us. Government redistribution of wealth is now accepted as "normal" (does anyone really question the legitimacy of welfare or Social Security any more?), even though it is completely unconstitutional.

I would like to suggest that the same thing has occurred in the church. But instead of *wealth redistribution* taking place, we might say that *responsibility redistribution* is occurring. For example, instead of parents willingly and gladly assuming the responsibility to teach their own children as the Scripture

---

[46] *People-Centered Evangelism* (Nashville: Broadman Press, 1971), 47.

commands (see Deuteronomy 6 and Ephesians 6), they have handed that job over to the church, whose paid professionals are only too eager to help. The only problem is that, just as wealth redistribution is wrong (since it involves taking your money through government coercion and simply giving it to someone else), so responsibility redistribution is wrong (since in involves parents surrendering to others their own God-mandated duty to raise their children in the nurture and admonition of the Lord).

Both approaches, it seems to me, are based on flawed assumptions. Take welfare, for example. Most of our politicians assume that the federal government has legal authority to create or administer a welfare program. (I say "most," because there are some like Ron Paul who think quite differently.) However, Congress has only those powers that are explicitly granted to it by the U. S. Constitution. If you read the Constitution with an unbiased mind you will be forced to conclude that there is absolutely no federal authority whatsoever for welfare programs. Yet government employs us, feeds us, regulates us, and now claims to be able to solve our problems. For many Americans, the state has become their church, and the federal government has become an idol, stripping individuals and communities of their social responsibilities and engaging in the unconstitutional transfer of wealth. And since the New Deal, a trickle has become a flood. To no one's surprise, Congress's latest proposal to revamp Social Security provides no systematic justification for involving government in social welfare. The reason is obvious. There can be no justification given for the state usurping the function of private individuals and the church. I agree with Ron Paul that "the federal welfare state is neither moral nor constitutional."[47] The tragedy is that American Christianity has so closely allied itself with the government of the day that the transcendent Gospel has become submerged in the world's values.

---

[47] http://www.lewrockwell.com/paul/paul80.html.

"But," you say, "if government doesn't take care of these people, who will?" The Bible teaches it is the *church's job* to fulfill Paul's injunction to "do good to all men" by helping non-Christians in need – feeding the hungry, clothing the naked, housing the homeless, healing the sick. And no believer is exempt from this task (see Luke 3:11; 1 John 3:17; James 1:27). On the other hand, no Scripture supports an active government role in alleviating poverty or the use of coercive measures. Paul even refused to command believers to help their less fortunate brothers, stating: "Each one of you should give whatever you have determined in your heart to give, not reluctantly or under compulsion, since God loves a cheerful giver" (2 Cor. 9:7).

Now let's apply these same principles to Christian education. Many parents have abdicated their responsibility to nurture their children and to teach them the things of God. As a result, the church has stepped in to provide a whole host of programs designed to compensate for the parents' inactivity – Nursery, Children's Church, Youth Ministry, Sunday School. The only problem is that these programs are unscriptural. They are also, by and large, ineffective. It is the home, and not the church, that is the God-ordained seat of Christian education. Why, then, should the church make it easy for parents to abdicate their job? Why, in other words, should the church encourage *responsibility redistribution*? In our day, parents seem to be busy with everything except the personal discipleship of their children. There's got to be a better way. In fact there is. *We can get off the church welfare dole and begin to build strong families.* When that happens, the church itself will be the greatest beneficiary.

Whose Responsibility Is It to Admonish the Unruly?

Let's take another example of responsibility redistribution, this time the matter of "church discipline." If there is one thing the New Testament clearly teaches, it is that brotherhood supersedes hierarchy (see Matthew 23). And it is in direct harmony with this teaching of Jesus that Paul commands the "brothers" in Thessalonica – not the church leaders – to carry out pastoral functions:

> We encourage you, brothers and sisters, to admonish the unruly, comfort the discouraged, and uphold the weak. Be patient with all (1 Thess. 5:14).

I well recall how shocked I was when I first realized that Paul was exhorting, not the leaders, but the brothers to "admonish the unruly." Yet the New Testament consistently downplays the role of elders in matters of church discipline. Every time Paul wrote to a church in order to deal with its problems, he never appealed to the leaders. Instead, his constant request was for the whole church to deal with its own troubles. 1 Corinthians is a good example of this. Here was perhaps the most troubled church in the entire New Testament, and yet Paul appealed to the entire assembly to handle its own problems. Thus he exhorts the whole church to discipline a disobedient member by handing him over to Satan (1 Corinthians 5). This is not to say that church leaders did not exist in Corinth, or in Thessalonica for that matter. In 1 Thessalonians 5:12-13 Paul calls upon the believers to duly recognize and esteem the leadership of others. He emphasizes that the leaders' authority was from the Lord, and he admonishes the Thessalonian Christians to appreciate them because of the importance of the work they were doing. But Paul does not tell the leaders to do *all* the admonishing. This is entirely consistent with Paul's teaching that every member of the Body of Christ is gifted, has ministry, and is responsible for pastoral care (Rom. 12:6; 1 Cor. 12:1ff.; Eph. 4:7).

As a result, the idea that only the elders may direct the affairs of a church or handle its problems is completely alien to Paul's thought. By contrast, he calls on the whole church (the "brothers and sisters") to:

- edify one another (Rom. 14:19; cf. 1 Thess. 5:11b)
- love one another (Rom. 13:8; cf. 1 Thess. 4:9)

- be devoted to one another (Rom. 12:10)
- admonish one another (Rom. 15:14)
- discipline fallen members (1 Cor. 5:3-5; 6:1-6)
- organize their own affairs (1 Cor. 11:33-34; 14:39-40; 16:2-3)
- abound in care for one another (1 Cor. 12:25)
- do the work of the Lord (1 Cor. 15:58)
- serve one another (Gal. 5:13)
- bear one another's burdens (Gal. 6:2)
- put up with one another (Eph. 4:2; Col. 3:13)
- show kindness and compassion to one another (Eph. 4:32)
- teach one another (Col. 3:16)
- encourage one another (1 Thess. 5:11a)
- admonish the unruly (1 Thess. 5:14)
- comfort the discouraged (1 Thess. 5:14)
- uphold the weak (1 Thess. 5:14)
- exhort one another (Heb. 3:13; 10:25)
- stir up one another to love and good works (Heb. 10:24)

Oftentimes believers who go to church regularly and profess to read their Bibles seem completely ignorant of their responsibilities. They say, "That's the preacher's job," failing to realize that the apostle Paul would have vehemently disagreed with them. It is *your* responsibility to "admonish the unruly," he says. Paul is literally referring to "those who are disorderly," that is, those who are out of step with the Word of God. In Thessalonica, it meant those people who had quit working because they expected the Lord to come at any moment. These believers were mooching off the gifts of others and were unwilling to support themselves. "Admonish them," says the apostle. Don't let them continue in their sin. Tell them to mend their ways. Don't do this in a mean-spirited way (Gal. 6:1), but point out to them that their behavior is unacceptable. We must rid our minds permanently of the notion that only a certain class of believers can be admonishers in the Body of Christ. Every Christian should labor to be a means of correction and reproof.[48]

Every Member a Minister

Unfortunately, we have become caught up in the whirl of professionalization that characterizes the ministry. There is one Book, and one Book alone, that can cure us of dangerous deceptions. Specifically, I am referring to a very basic truth about ministry that many of us have forgotten – in part or in whole – in the church today. It is that every child of God is a minister. I am not just referring to that individual who has felt a "call" to enter "the" ministry. Everyone who is a genuine disciple of Jesus Christ *has* entered the ministry. The Bible knows nothing about a Christian who is not also a minister (see Rom 12:3-8; 1 Cor. 12-14). Another way of putting this is to say that, according to the Scriptures, there is no clergy-laity distinction. Again, this may come as a shock and a surprise to those of us who are accustomed to referring to certain individuals in the church as a "reverend" or a "clergyman." The Word of God knows nothing of a "ministry of the clergy" on the one hand, and a "ministry of the laity" on the other. The simple truth is that all of God's

---

[48] Interestingly, mutual participation has enjoyed a long history in Baptist life. According to Wayne E. Ward, "The Worship of God," *The People of God: Essays on the Believers' Church*, eds. Paul Basden and David S. Dockery (Nashville: Broadman Press, 1991), 68, the first Baptist churches in England "were trying to restore the primitive apostolic form of the church, and, with unerring logic, they understood that worship must be an outward expression of their ecclesiology. Since the 'gathered community of believers' was their basic concept of church, all forms of worship, including baptism, the Lord's Supper, prayers, hymns, Scripture exposition, confession, and receiving forgiveness, involved full congregational participation." This seems a far cry from the spectatorism so prevalent in Baptist churches today.

"clergy" are laypeople, and all of God's "laypeople" are clergy. This is not to deny the fact that there were pastors/elders/overseers in the primitive Christian community. There were pastors, but they were also a part of the *laos* – the "people" of God (Phil. 1:1-2). The New Testament knows no separate existence of pastors apart from the rest of the Christian community.

You ask, "Why, then, do we have certain men who are authorized to officiate at church?" Bible history helps us here. In Old Testament times, God did indeed have a special "clergy" as it were, centered in the tribe of Levi. The members of that tribe had been elevated to the status of what we might call today a "professional ministry." This was made clear in several ways: by their right to encamp between the body of the nation and the sanctuary where God dwelt; by their privilege to touch holy things that others were not permitted to handle; by their exclusive right to bear the ark; by their special garbs; and, perhaps above all, by their being separated from the people (the *laos*) in whose behalf they offered sacrifices and offerings unto God. But we are not to gather from these patterns that God's people today are to have a clergy-laity distinction. The cross of Christ forever abolished all such distinctions, with the result that today every person who has been purged and purified by the blood of Jesus is a priest of God (Rev. 1:6). We are poles apart from our apostolic forefathers at this point, even when we confess our faith in their words. Yet despite all its stress on elders, the New Testament never lets us lose sight of the priesthood of all believers.

This is what is so injurious about those who would claim a special status from God in the church today. Perhaps it is time to put the names of the real ministers on the signboard out front and upon our official letterheads: EVERY MEMBER. You say, "The 'minister' will become jealous for his position and the honor of his office!" Might I say in response: if your minister is so jealous of his "high office," he has forgotten that his true occupation is to prepare the saints to carry out the work of the ministry to the building up of the Body of Christ (Eph. 4:11-12). Not only so, but if that is his understanding of ministry, he shows himself disqualified to fulfill the role he assumes. Is it true that God has made me a priest unto himself? If so, certain questions arise: Why do I allow others to do all the work? Could an observer learn from the quality of my service that I am a minister in my church every bit as much as the overseers are? Why do I ever allow myself to exalt mere human beings so that Jesus is no longer acknowledged as the one true Head of the Church (Col. 1:18)?

When I was a part of the Jesus Movement in Hawaii, I thought it best to leave the institutionalized church – I and many others who were dissatisfied with the talk the church was doing, with no action. As much as I could, I wanted to find out what God had to say about his church and this led my back to the Scriptures themselves. And God, for his part, began to bring me back into a vital relationship with the local church. I discovered that God's basic call was to mission – to engage in a redemptive task in the world. He was calling a people who would give their all, even their lives if necessary, to join with him in this redemptive task. He said to his church, "You shall be to me a kingdom of priests" – men and women who understood who God is and what God is about in the world. I came to understand that this mission is both personal and social. The priesthood of all believers means that since every believer is a priest, every Christian is called to be a minister and has a ministry. Thus, the call to salvation and the call to ministry are one and the same. Young people who struggle with the question of whether God has called them into "the" ministry are asking, it seems to me, the wrong question. For if a person has been called by God to be a Christian, then he or she has also been called into the ministry. This is, in fact, how God fulfills his mission in the world. He calls every Christian to mission and the Christian, in turn, fulfills that mission through their ministry. This means that the primary responsibility for carrying out God's mission in the world is not that of the "clergy" but of the *laos* – the entire people of God. We cannot, therefore, slough off our "ministry" to others and just pay the salary of the "clergy" or the "missionary." We all have a responsibility in addition to the giving of our money.

This leads me to another important aspect of mission: its social dimension. If God's mission in the world is to be accomplished, then his ministers – the *laos* – are to carry out their ministry *in the world*. To "believe" in Christ means to join him in what he is seeking to do in the world. It is for this reason that Christ gave pastors to the church (Eph. 4:11-12). He calls them to equip the saints – his basic ministers – for their ministry, and in this way the Body of Christ is built up both by the addition of new "cells" to the Body (evangelism) but also by the nourishing of existing "cells" (edification). This equipping ministry of pastors is of unique importance and must be undertaken with the utmost dedication. If the church is failing to advance the mission of God in the world, it may be because we have been relying upon the wrong people to be his ministers. God has called every believer to be a minister, and his people are to be equipped for this call.

If, then, the ministry of the *laos* is God's means of fulfilling his mission in the world, it is necessary that we view what we do on Sunday as merely the beginning, not the climax, of our work. In other words, we need to change the basis for evaluating the effectiveness of the ministry of our churches. The question is not "How many attended on Sunday?" but "What did those who attended on Sunday do during the week to advance Christ's kingdom?" This is what it means to be the People of God. It is a people who understand that the mission of the church is to fulfill God's redemptive mission. Our calling is to join God's army and become aggressively involved in his mission in the world. The point is that God's call to salvation and his call to mission are one and the same. To follow Christ in this way is not optional for the one who is truly "born again." It is to this life of mission that we must respond. Not only is this possible and practical in this day of over-professionalization; an emphasis on anything else is a perversion of the Gospel.

From Serve Us to Service

We see, then, that the people we call "ministers" are not appointed by Christ to do the work for the members, but to prepare them for their work, so that the whole church may be built up. The grace that saves also grants power for ministry. Indeed, only on the basis of the ministry of all Christians has God promised that the church can reach maturity (4:11-16). What, then, is the role of the pastor? Pastors are God's change agents for the flow of dynamic energy for spiritual growth. They are not CEOs but catalysts for equipping the saints. "Equipping the saints" is, in fact, the heart of the pastoral ministry. Spending time and energy on other things is a misuse of that calling.

This is precisely where so many pastors struggle. Rather than following the biblical principles and patterns of New Testament church leadership, their tendency is to acquiesce to the expectations of their peers, thus promoting the unbiblical division of God's people into an elite class of "ministers" and a vast second-class body of believers known as "laypeople." Rather than encouraging and teaching each part to do its work in the Body, they pile responsibilities on a few with special gifts for organization or promotion. As a result, the institutionalized church blinds believers to many potentially kingdom-building ministries. The solution to the problem is to understand that *each* believer has received grace for ministry, and that ministry is for *all* believers. The basic point of Ephesians 4:1-16 is that a true New Testament model of ministry involves all the people of God who, by the grace and power of God, are free to serve in the work of the kingdom of God. It underscores the need for those entrusted with leadership to equip all believers for the work of the ministry. Indeed, the chief priority of pastoral leadership is discipling men and women for the kingdom.

Following the Ephesians 4 model of ministry will not be easy in a day of religious professionals. One of the greatest obstacles to genuine renewal is the institutionalized church itself. In the spirit of the Old Testament, the church has set up a professional priesthood that feeds the "superstar" idea. The contemporary church makes little room for spiritual gifts and fails to appreciate "God's varied grace" that is manifested when all the gifts are affirmed and operate cooperatively. Pastors have not been taught that the function of local church leadership is to identify and awaken these gifts that are dormant within the community of believers. If we would take every-member ministry seriously, as was done in the early Christian church, the dull picture of our contemporary churches would be radically altered. Instead of churches designed for "preacher function," they would intentionally promote "body function." Formal teaching would be accompanied by informal teaching. Every member would contribute to the success of the Body. Pastor-dependency would be replaced by mutual edification. By serving one another in love, we would begin to create satisfying and lasting relationships with each other. And as the Body obeys its Head, Jesus Christ, it "grows and builds itself up in love, as each part does its job" (Eph. 4:15-16).

It is worth pausing for a moment to contemplate how glorious this truth is. The Body of Christ is a wonderful thing. It is where Jesus dwells. It is where he continues to do what he began in the Gospels (Acts 1:1). Still today, Jesus is at work in and through his Body. Few New Testament writings describe this Body as completely as does Paul's first letter to the Corinthians. There Paul shows how the Body of Christ is based on, and flows out of, the unity and diversity of the Triune God. In 1 Corinthians 12:4-6 Paul says that the Spirit grants to all the members of the Body spiritual gifts (*charismata*). The Son, on the other hand, assigns ministries (*diakoniai*) to every gifted member. These are opportunities to exercise one's spiritual gifts in ways that edify other believers. Note that God does not give us gifts so that we might simply boast or brag of them. God desires us to serve and to use those gifts as the Lord Jesus directs us and in the place of his appointment. Finally, Paul says that God himself grants us the *energemata* – the power – to use our spiritual gifts in an effective way.

We must never forget this. All who are born of the Spirit of God are members of Christ's Body on this earth. In each one of us the Spirit has come to dwell. To each one of us he has given a gift, which Paul calls a "manifestation of the Spirit" (v. 7). This truth is foundational to all we do as the people of God. For if we neglect Paul's teaching on gifts, the church becomes just another organization. Everything is done to operate and build the organization, and all our energy is poured into that. But we must never think of the church as a human organization that operates programs on behalf of its membership. The biblical church functions when its members are using their infinite variety of abilities and aptitudes for mutual edification.

This is the divine blueprint for the church, and many believers today are rediscovering it. They are realizing that just as economic freedom is an essential requisite for political freedom, so spiritual freedom is a requisite for the Body of Christ to operate according to God's design. The "fecundity of freedom" that made America the greatest nation in the nineteenth century succeeded for one main reason. It enabled people to cooperate with each other without coercion or central direction. By dispersing power, the free market provided an offset to political power. Undoubtedly, the main source of the economic revolution was private initiative operating in a free market open to all. People received little help from the government, but they also experienced little interference from the government. The narrowly limited government of the nineteenth century had little concentrated power that endangered the ordinary man.

As we have seen, all of this changed with the Great Depression. The Depression was widely interpreted as a failure of free market capitalism. That myth led to a new vision of America. Emphasis on personal responsibility was replaced by emphasis on the person as a pawn controlled by forces beyond his or her control. Government increasingly undertook the task of taking from some to give to others in the name of security and equality. One government policy after another was established to regulate our pursuits. I believe these developments were produced with good intentions. But even the strongest supporters of the welfare state would agree that the results have been disappointing. Americans no longer have a "can do" mentality. The human freedom proclaimed so eloquently in the Declaration of Independence is today a bare shell of what it once was. And today, as we clamor for the government to "serve us," a new class of "civil servants" spends larger and larger fractions of our income supposedly on our behalf.

Fortunately, the tide is turning. In America there is a growing recognition of the dangers of big government. This shift in thinking is being reflected not only in the political sphere, but also in the religious one. There is a budding Christian subculture that is beginning to take Paul's teaching on spiritual gifts seriously. For them, the work of the church is not something to be done by hired professionals. It is more than running meetings and perhaps doing a little missionary outreach. It is more than teaching Sunday school and heading up committees. The church is a Body in which the Spirit of God has distributed gifts to every member.

This is an amazing truth. It means that there are no insignificant members in the Body of Christ. It is not just those who lead our "worship services" that have gifts. Each believer has the ability to do something to encourage, strengthen, and help other Christians. We are only fooling ourselves if we think that because we can't preach or teach or lead we are not a member of the Body. When we see the church as Paul sees it, we will stop thinking that only the teachers or leaders are important. We will see that the Triune God has designed the Body with beautiful balance. No one person has all the gifts. No one person can do it all. This is the message of Paul; this is the message of the New Testament.

Every Member a Missionary

Let us consider, finally, the privilege that every believer has of being a missionary. The earliest Christians did not talk about witnessing. They told others about Jesus. The book of Acts shows us how the church moved beyond cultural differences to embrace people regardless of their race, nationality, and circumstances. The proof was in the *doing*. It is true that the apostles (such as Paul) did much of the witnessing in the early church. But most of it was done by the rest of the believers – plain, ordinary Christians reaping God's harvest. In Antioch of Syria they witnessed to both Jews and Greeks and many believed. In obedience to Jesus' command they had gone out as witnesses instead of waiting for the world to come to them. God was moving his people into action, and as a result "The word of God continued to spread and multiply" (Acts 12:24).

I wish I could tell you that I have introduced thousands to the Lord Jesus. I can't. And those I have had the joy of seeing come to faith have sometimes been left orphaned. But I have come to see that my primary vocation – my main "business" in life – is the Gospel business, the work of discipleship. *Today* is the day of salvation, and those of us who possess the Gospel *have* to share it. To be in the kingdom business means crucifying self and serving others. It means helping the neglected, bearing each others' burdens, blessing those who persecute you, serving faithfully according to your gifts, and overcoming evil with good. This is especially important in light of the hour. The days are evil, and Christ's return may be near. When Christ is in control, everything in life is different. Our one goal is to live in a manner worthy of the Gospel. We serve him without complaining. We would gladly lose everything for his sake. We forget our past failures and press on toward the goal of being formed in him. "To know him and to make him known" becomes our only passion.

If every Christian is called to be a witness, and if every church has a global mission at its door, why are only certain

people called "missionaries," and why do boards and agencies try
to do the work of the local church? There is not a single hint in
the New Testament that the early Christians saw evangelism as
the responsibility of certain professionals. Of course, people and
agencies that work with and through the local church may be
said to be fulfilling their mission responsibility. But in reality,
every one of us ought to be a "fulltime missionary." Jesus
himself was the ultimate missionary, and he entrusted world
missions to his followers. And even if we cannot travel to a
foreign field, the "uttermost parts of the world" have come to
us. Just look at any college or university campus today.
Missiologists call this "global missions in reverse," but it is no
less missions. Rodney Clapp, in his influential book *A Peculiar
People*, writes:

> In the light of Christianity as a new culture we can
> properly hear and understand Jesus' Great
> Commission. These are actually not words that
> comport at all with Constantinianism and revivalistic
> approaches to evangelism. What Jesus calls for is
> not a simple conveyance of information, not a mere
> inward acknowledgement, but a making of disciples
> from all nations and a teaching them "to obey
> everything I have commanded you" (Mt 28:18-20).
> In our terms, he calls for the induction of people
> into a different way of life – and so a departure, in
> one fashion and then another, from old ways of life
> that formerly defined them and made them what
> they are.[49]

Speaking personally, I look back with awe at the mileposts
God used in preparing me for my present responsibilities as a
global missionary, from meeting missionaries and missions-
minded people while growing up in Hawaii, to missionary

---

[49] Rodney Clapp, *A Peculiar People* (Downers Grove: InterVarsity, 1996),
166-67.

training in Wheaton with Greater Europe Mission's Eurocorps team, to sharing my faith as a student in Basel, to preaching in such varied places as India and Korea. At the same time, I cannot and dare not lose sight of my "home mission field" of Southside Virginia, where the cultural and social barriers can be just as real as those in Africa or Asia. A thrilling part of being evangelistic is seeing people of different citizenships becoming citizens of the kingdom of God and missionaries themselves. I like to think that whatever work I do in my career as a professor and author, my ultimate task is to equip others to carry on Christ's mission. And I mean all Christians, not just those who are professionally trained.

Are you, then, a minister of the Gospel? Are you creating cynicism or compassion by your actions? Are you heartbroken that countless people have never experienced the forgiveness of their sins? Or that their condition is wretched? Will you do whatever is needed in order to fulfill your commitment to God? In short, are you a missionary – locally, regionally, globally, even cross-culturally (see Acts 1:8)? I think it's very dangerous when we'd rather be good businessmen or pastors or scholars or homeschoolers than good witnesses for Jesus. I think it's very dangerous when we find good reasons for hiding our faith. I think it's very dangerous when we learn how to be "all things to all men" but not for the purpose of "saving some." Thus we no longer speak about "conversion" because it would offend and shock people. How easy it is to get sidetracked, thinking that Jesus came to establish the power of the state or social justice. What is the point of Christianity if not to lead men and women to acknowledge Jesus Christ as their Savior and Lord? Why does the church exist if not for the conversion of the lost?

I'm not speaking of driving a wedge between the evangelistic mandate and the cultural mandate, as if the Gospel does not penetrate every aspect of life. To me it's a matter of priorities. For many today, Christianity consists in joining a church or playing politics. We are acting like the church is a social club or a political party. I'm not against involvement in politics, but success in politics is not the goal of life. For the Christian, politics is at best an accessory. In the Beatitudes our Lord put politics in its place, stripped it of its prestige, and emptied it of spiritual value and meaning. Instead, he taught that as we humble ourselves before God and reject all earthly standards of success and happiness we learn to view the world as he sees it. We then want to make Jesus and his teachings known as far and wide as possible. We learn that the way of the Gospel is the way of suffering, trial, poverty, and sometimes despair. We no longer cling to our creature comforts. We are ready to sacrifice everything for the Gospel. It becomes the object of our preoccupation. It gives meaning to all of life. We now find the true significance of our earthly existence. We learn to accept the insecurity of freedom in God. We do not need security! We are free in Christ to live for God's glory, not our own. Paul sums up the whole emphasis of the Gospel-centered life in a well-known passage in 2 Corinthians 4:1-6:

> Therefore, since we have this ministry, and because we have received mercy, we don't become discouraged. Instead, we have renounced hidden and shameful things. We don't resort to craftiness or handle the word of God deceitfully. But by manifesting the truth, we commend ourselves to everyone's conscience in the sight of God.
>
> So even if our Gospel is veiled, it is veiled to those who are perishing, whose minds the god of this world has blinded, who don't believe lest the light of the Gospel of the glory of Christ, who is the image of God, should shine on them.
>
> For we don't preach ourselves but Christ Jesus the Lord. We are your servants for Jesus' sake. For that reason the God who commanded light to shine out of darkness has shone in our hearts so that we may

bring to light the knowledge of God's glory in the
face of Jesus Christ.

It seems to me, then, that bearing witness to Christ is
absolutely and unavoidably necessary and obligatory for the
believer. This conclusion is not based on experience or
philosophy. It is based on the totality of God's missionary
mandate. And it is at the very core of the Jesus paradigm.

The Community of the Spirit:
Leadership Jesus' Style

Must the pastor be a superstar?

Howard Snyder[50]

Leadership is only worthy of allegiance when the led
freely grant it to the leader in response to the leader's
servant posture.

Donald Kraybill[51]

How's Your Hekastology?

Paul's letter to the Ephesians pulsates with theology. It treats
such majestic themes as the grace of God, predestination,
reconciliation, the sovereignty of God, justification and
sanctification, and the church as the Body of Christ. It is a grave
mistake, however, to think that the theology of Ephesians is
limited to these topics. A note of "Hekastology" pervades the
letter. Let me explain.

Throughout the book of Ephesians Paul shows how God is
working out his plan of salvation by calling men and women to
Christ and forming them into a new redeemed society called the
church. The blessings of salvation come to us in keeping with
the eternal purpose of God, "according to which he has chosen
us" (1:4). Note that salvation has its origin in the gracious choice

---

[50] *The Problem of Wineskins* (Downers Grove: InterVarsity, 1975), 81.

[51] *The Upside-Down Kingdom* (Scottsdale, PA: Herald, 2003), 238.

of God. Thus Paul emphasizes the utter helplessness of humanity and God's gracious and sovereign choice of individual sinners to be saved in and through Christ. Believing Gentiles, along with believing Jews, are now being built into a great spiritual structure "upon the foundation of the apostles and prophets, Christ Jesus himself being the cornerstone" (2:20). Christ alone (and not any pastor or church leader) supports and holds together both the foundation and the walls, and it is he who gives to this spiritual edifice its unity and strength.

In the second part of the letter Paul deals more specifically with how members of this new edifice are to "walk" (a Jewish metaphor that describes Christian living). Rather than remaining spiritual infants, believers are to mature in their Christian life. In particular, Paul shows how God has provided for the growth of his church by bestowing various gifts upon his believing people. Christians are to perform two kinds of ministry. In relation to the world, they have a missionary task to make disciples of all the nations. In relation to one another, they are to recognize and use their gifts for the edification (building up) of the church. Each member of the Body of Christ is to do his or her part in this task until the church attains "the measure of the stature of the fullness of Christ" (4:13).

In 4:11 we learn that believers who are endowed with gifts by Christ are themselves gifts to the whole Body of Christ. The apostles and prophets are mentioned first, as through them God gave guidance and direction to his people in the early years of the church.[52] Evangelists and pastors continue that work. Evangelists may be considered as missionaries to the unconverted who possess an unusual power in recommending the Gospel to others. Pastors function both to shepherd the

---

[52] Of course, both "apostle" and "prophet" may be used in a broader, less-technical sense of general church leaders today. We might think of the modern missionary as having an apostolic function. Who the "prophet" is today is more open to debate. For an excellent discussion, see Howard A. Snyder, *The Community of the King* (Downers Grove: InterVarsity, 2004), 103-09.

flock of God and to instruct them in divine truth. Incidentally, this is the only place in the entire New Testament where the term "pastor" is used to describe church leaders. Elsewhere they are called "overseers" (Acts 20:28; 1 Tim 3:2) and "elders" (Acts 20:17; 1 Pet 5:1). Paul says it is the task of the apostles, prophets, evangelists, and pastors to "build up the body of Christ" (4:12). This is accomplished not only by such gifted individuals teaching the Word of God but also by each believer employing the "gift of grace" that God has given him or her (4:7). As far as the goal of edification is concerned, Paul says that every believer has a contribution to make. Paul pictures the church as an organism in which each member contributes to the growth of the whole, a process that takes place "as each and every part does its job effectively" (4:16).

Notice how Paul addresses himself deliberately to "every" believer. The Greek word for "every" is *hekastos* – hence "Hekastology." This isn't just an insignificant detail. Paul seeks to drive home the truth that *every* believer has a special service in the church. Every saint is to make his or her own contribution to the mission and unity of the church, all cooperating according to their ability. This truth is also evident in 1 Corinthians 14:26: "When you assemble, everyone [*hekastos*] has a psalm, teaching, revelation, another language, or interpretation. All things must be done for edification." Unfortunately, many Christians meet together on Sunday without ever "assembling" as the Body of Christ in this manner. But Paul is clear: every believer has a ministry, and everyone is to participate and give to others what God has given them. The same principle is stated in Hebrews 10:24-25: "We must consider how to stimulate one another to love and good works. We should not forget to assemble ourselves together, as some of you are doing. Instead, we must continue to encourage each other even more, as we see the Day of the Lord approaching." Here the purpose of gathering together as the Body of Christ is made crystal clear: mutual ministry. The emphasis is not on where we so often put it ("go to church!") but rather on the truth that each of us should minister to the others when we come together as a group. In most of our churches, this is not allowed and not possible. Ask yourself: Is your assembly a place where Christians are stirring up one another to love and helpful deeds? Is it a place where people are free to admonish, warn, and encourage one another? And are you a participant or merely an observer? In other words, how's your Hekastology?

There's Only One "Senior Pastor"

How, then, can we purge our thinking from unbiblical concepts of ministry? I'll cast my mite into the treasury by offering some basic reflections on three essential but often overlooked passages. The first is 1 Peter 5:1-4.

> I appeal to the elders who are among you – I who am a fellow elder, a witness of Christ's sufferings, and one who will share in the glory that will be revealed: Shepherd the flock of God that is among you, serving as overseers, not because you have to but because you want to, not for dishonest gain but eagerly, not by lording it over those entrusted to you but by being examples to the flock to follow. Then, when the Chief Shepherd appears, you will receive the crown of glory that does not fade away.

When Peter wrote these words, most people were thoroughly familiar with sheep and shepherding (as they are today in places like Africa). Elders, he says, are like shepherds who guard the flock under the tender supervision of the Chief Shepherd. They feed the sheep with God's Word and lead them by example. They keep the sheep from wandering off into pastures that might harm them. Theirs is an enormous task, but faithful elders will reap the reward of an unfading crown of glory, awarded by the Chief Shepherd himself.

Of course, if anyone could have assumed the title "Senior Pastor," it was the apostle Peter. From the Gospels we learn that he occupied a privileged position among Jesus' disciples. Along with the sons of Zebedee and his brother Andrew he belonged to the intimate circle of those who gathered about our Lord. According to Mark 1:16, he was one of the first disciples Jesus called. Mark 5:37 explicitly notes that Jesus permitted no one else to enter the house of the ruler of the synagogue except Peter and the sons of Zebedee.

Even within the innermost circle of disciples, it is Peter who always stands in the foreground. He alone attempts to imitate his Master in walking on the water. He alone is the spokesman for the Twelve. When Jesus directs a question to all the disciples, it is Peter who answers (Mark 8:29ff.). At the transfiguration it was Peter who proposed that they erect tents (Mark 9:5). It is he who asks the questions all the disciples want answered (Matt. 18:21). In Luke 22:8 Peter and John are directed to prepare the Passover. The lists of the disciples all give Peter the first place. The list in Matthew 10:2 actually calls him the "first" (Greek *protos*). After the resurrection the angel says, "Go and tell his disciples *and Peter* that he is going ahead of you into Galilee" (Mark 16:7). It is Peter who defends the cause of the Gospel when the Jerusalem authorities take action against the apostles (Acts 4:8; 5:29). Especially in Mark's Gospel is the preeminent position of Peter emphasized, in keeping with the solid tradition that Mark is a *viva voce* transcription of Peter's teaching in Rome.[53]

No one can deny the special role Peter played among Jesus' apostles. Isn't it striking, then, that Peter refers to himself in 1 Peter 5:1, not as a "senior" or "superior" elder, but simply as a "fellow elder" (Greek *sumpresbuteros*)? Or that he tells his fellow elders not to lord it over those entrusted to them (5:3)? Or that he calls Jesus the "Chief Shepherd" (i.e., Senior Pastor) of the sheep (5:4)? This should not surprise us at all. There is an utter and complete absence of any notion of a priestly caste in the New Testament. The early Christian assemblies had no holy

---

[53] See my book *Why Four Gospels?* (Grand Rapids: Kregel, 2001) for a defense of this view.

man, no head honcho, no top gun, no "clergy" to lead the pack. Clergy dominance came much later and postdates the New Testament by at least a generation. James Dunn, one of the world's leading New Testament scholars, has noted, "Increasing institutionalism is the clearest mark of early Catholicism – when church becomes increasingly identified with institution, when authority becomes increasingly coterminous with office, when a basic distinction between clergy and laity becomes increasingly self-evident, when grace becomes increasingly narrowed to well-defined ritual acts. We saw above that such features were absent from first generation Christianity, though in the second the picture was beginning to change."[54]

How far have we departed from the simplicity that is in Christ! The apostles were very specific in conveying the precise meaning of leadership. It was not, in Peter's words, to involve "lording it over" the flock, as if we were superior to others. It was to be a leadership of lowly service (1 Pet. 5:3). I hope the truth of the matter will someday no longer be a subject of debate and confusion among God's people. The whole traditional concept of one pastor of a local congregation is a practice that is absolutely foreign to Scripture. Overseeing elders are appointed by the Owner of the Sheep to exercise humble, non-authoritarian leadership among – not over – them. Thus no church ministered to by a "top gun" can be said to be a truly New Testament church. The only "top gun" in the New Testament was Diotrephes, who "loved to be first" and wanted to be boss, and such a leader was condemned by the apostle John (3 John 9-10).

The time has come to bring our local church practices under the scrutiny of God's Word. If there are practices in our tradition that are in conflict with the New Testament revelation, then we have only one option, and that is to correct our practices. The Bible clearly rejects our clergy-laity divide. All

---

[54] James Dunn, *Unity and Diversity in the New Testament* (London: SCM, 2006), 351.

members of the local church are to function in the body according to the grace given unto them (Rom. 12:1-8). The church is a temple in which every Christian is a priest who offers spiritual sacrifices to God (1 Pet. 2:5, 9). According to the New Testament, all Christians do the work of ministry through the exercise of spiritual gifts. Whatever legitimate distinction can be made between leaders and led (e.g., 1 Thess. 5:12-13) does not negate the fundamental truth of the priesthood of all believers.

It seems to me that it is an affront to Jesus Christ for any pastor to assume a place of prominence and uniqueness when Jesus himself condemned any attempt at superiority of position (Matt. 23:8). Jesus is the only Senior Pastor of the church. The rest of us are brothers. R. T. France, in his Tyndale Commentary on Matthew, reminds us that "[Jesus] has the only true claim to 'Moses' seat.' Over against that unique authority His disciples must avoid the use of honorific titles for one another, an exhortation which today's church could profitably take more seriously, not only in relation to formal ecclesiastical titles ('Most Rev.', 'my Lord Bishop,' etc.) but more significantly in its excessive deference to academic qualifications or to authoritative status in the churches."[55] Many of our man-made approaches to doing church are open to blame precisely because they never get down to this level. True Christian discipleship is always countercultural. One of the clearest indications of this is Jesus' insistence that the one who wants to be first must be the slave of all, that greatness comes in service, and that giving your life away is the only way to find it (Mark 10:44-45).

Let me flesh this out in four ways. If you are a church leader, might I suggest in the first place that you take down the diplomas hanging on your office wall? No one in your congregation is even faintly impressed by them (I dare say, not even you should be). Second, recognize that biblical eldership has no room for religious titles or exalted positions like "senior

---

[55] R. T. France, *Matthew: An Introduction and Commentary* (Downers Grove: InterVarsity, 2007), 325.

pastor," "associate pastor," "reverend," and the like. If you need a title, "elder" or "brother" will do just fine. Third, if you do hold to the "one man pastor" concept, get rid of it. Only the shared leadership model is taught in the New Testament, for only shared leadership promotes the New Covenant priesthood through manifesting Christ as the only true Head of the church (Col. 1:18). Finally, commit yourself to going back to the Bible in all that you do. Everything in the Christian life needs to be built upon the Word of God.

Church Leadership According to Philippians 1:1

Next, we turn to Philippians 1:1, where we note that Paul greets "all the saints in Christ Jesus who are in Philippi, along with the overseers and deacons." In the New Testament there are two Greek words that are used interchangeably to describe church leaders. The word *presbuteros* is usually rendered "elder," while the word *episkopos* is usually rendered "bishop" or "overseer." The uniform practice of the early church in the New Testament was to have a plurality of elders or overseers. This is because leadership by one person always tends to exalt one man over others, while the Bible clearly teaches that only Christ is to be exalted, for he alone is the Head of the church (Col. 1:15-20; Matt. 23:8-12). Thus Paul does not greet the "pastor" (singular) or the "overseer" (singular) of the church in Philippi, but the "overseers" (plural). Although the churches we attend may have a "pastor," this is not the teaching of the New Testament.

It is instructive that Paul describes these believers in Philippi, not as being "under" their leaders (in which case the Greek preposition would have been *hupo*) but rather "along with" (Greek *sun*) the overseers and deacons. This is not accidental. In terms of biblical teaching, there is no separate class of those who minister while others stand by and watch. Though some ministers may devote more of their time and energy to ministering to others, and some may even be paid for their ministry, all Christians are "in the ministry." As Alec Motyer of

Christ Church, England, writes: "Within the local church there was fellowship (all the saints) and leadership (the bishops and deacons). The leadership, however, was not an imposition upon the fellowship but an expansion of it. For the saints are not 'under' but *with* ('in company with') the bishops."[56] Motyer adds, "As is always the case in the Bible, the existence and activity of such ministries arise out of the needs of the church, and they can be exercised only in ways that are suited to what the church is. Thus, for example, the New Testament never speaks of any ministry as mediating between God and the church."[57] Motyer is referring to the great New Testament doctrine of the priesthood of all believers, which is an essential part of the biblical idea of the church.

It is also important to note that neither "overseers" nor "deacons" is used with the Greek definite article. This seems significant. In Greek, the use of the definite article generally points out particular identity, whereas the absence of the article generally emphasizes qualities or characteristics. Apparently Paul uses this construction to emphasize the work these individuals do, and not their titles. Evidence for this functional meaning of the terms comes from other Pauline epistles as well (see 1 Thess. 5:12-13; 1 Cor. 12:28-31; Rom. 12:6-8). The clear impression we receive is that of local churches under apostolic authority, with each church managing its own affairs under the leadership of those who oversee and serve the congregation.

The implications of this are tremendous. If you were to go into practically any Protestant church today, you would likely encounter a hard and fast clergy-laity distinction, and very often a church led (or ruled) by one man. Or you may find the leadership divided into pastors, elders, and deacons, or into ruling elders and teaching elders, with the ruling elders functioning more like administrators who are involved in very little pastoral ministry. None of these models is truly biblical.

---

[56] *The Message of Philippians* (Downers Grove: InterVarsity, 1984), 33.
[57] *Philippians*, 35.

While some passages suggest the presence of an elder who became the spokesman for the leadership, there is no suggestion anywhere of one man who was viewed as "the" pastor. Such a person was always accountable to the other elders and never led in a hierarchical manner, as was the case with Diotrephes (3 John 9-11). Thus the church is never viewed as a one-man team with the "pastor" doing all the work while the "laypeople" watched. Because of the limited capacity of one person to lead the church, New Testament leadership was plural and equal, with no system of hierarchy. Of course, certain people will generally function as leaders among the leaders because of their wisdom and experience, but all are equal and accountable to each other.

Moreover, in the worship of the church the leaders are never seen as dominating. Instead, a pattern of mutual participation by the congregation seems to have been the mark of all apostolic churches (see Rom. 12:4-8; 1 Cor. 14:26; Eph. 4:11-16; 5:19; Col. 3:16; Heb. 10:24-25; 1 Pet. 4:10-11), regardless of their geographical location (see 1 Cor. 4:16-17; 11:16; 14:33). The New Testament teaches that the congregational meeting is to be a place where *all* Christians exercise their spiritual gifts and stimulate one another to love and good deeds. In addition, the leaders in the congregation did not take upon themselves honorific titles that might set them apart from the rest of the "saints." Alexander Strauch, author of *Biblical Eldership*, correctly notes:

> There were prophets, teachers, apostles, pastors, evangelists, leaders, elders, and deacons within the early church, but these terms were not used as formal titles. For example, all Christians are saints, but there is no "Saint John." All are priests, but there is no "Priest Philip." Some are elders, but there is no "Elder Paul." Some are pastors, but there is no "Pastor James." Some are deacons, but there is no "Deacon Peter." Some are apostles, but is no "Apostle Andrew." Rather than gaining honor

though titles and position, New Testament believers received honor primarily for their service and work (Acts 15:26; Romans 16:1, 2, 4, 12; 1 Corinthians 8:18; 2 Corinthians 8:18; Philippians 2:29, 30; Colossians 1:7; 4:12, 13; 1 Thessalonians 5:12; 1 Timothy 3:1). The early Christians referred to each other by personal names – Timothy, Paul, Titus, etc. – or referred to an individual's spiritual character and work: "...Stephen, a man full of faith and of the Holy Spirit..." (Acts 6:5); Barnabas, "...a good man, and full of the Holy Spirit and of faith..." (Acts 11:24); "...Philip the evangelist..." (Acts 21:8); "Greet Prisca and Aquila, my fellow-workers in Christ Jesus" (Romans 16:3); "Greet Mary, who has worked hard for you" (Romans 16:6); etc. The array of ecclesiastical titles accompanying the names of Christian leaders today is completely missing from the New Testament, and would have appalled the apostles and early believers.[58]

In light of what we have said above, there is a great need for reformation within local churches in the way we view leadership. Traditional pastoral ministry promotes an unbiblical one-man model of leadership under the self-styled "pastor." In contrast, the New Testament teaches oversight by a plurality of men called elders. Some elders might be gifted differently and may even excel in specific pastoral tasks, but there is no biblical warrant for dividing church leaders into separate "offices" with honorific titles.

Traditional concepts of "pastor" are clearly unscriptural. The New Testament does not speak of two classes of Christians, as we do today. According to the Bible, all Christians are the people of God who through the exercise of spiritual gifts do the work

---

[58] Alexander Strauch, *Biblical Eldership* (Colorado Springs: Lewis and Roth, 1995), 259.

of the ministry. Such is the teaching of Paul in Philippians 1:1. Once again, Alec Motyer summarizes it well:

> How is leadership to be exercised? What is the relationship between leaders and led? The one word *with* provides the answer: '…the saints', writes Paul, '…with the bishops and deacons.' The strong natural leader chooses the easy path of being out front, taking it for granted that all will follow; the low-profile leader 'plays it cool', submerges his own identify and takes the risk that the tail will soon wag the dog. The more demanding exercise, the sterner discipline and the more rewarding way are found in companionate leadership, the saints *with* the overseers and deacons.

> This kind of leadership has many facets. It involves realizing that leader and led share the same Christian experience: both are sinners saved by the same precious blood, always and without distinction wholly dependent on the same patient mercy of God. It involves putting first whatever creates and maintains the unity of the Spirit in the bond of peace. It means that leaders see themselves first as members of the body, and only then as ministers. In this way they face every situation from within the local body of Christ and not as people dropped in from the outside (or even from above!). It involves patiently waiting for the Holy Spirit to grant unanimity to the church in making and executing plans. It involves open relationships in which the leaders do not scheme to get their own way or play off one against another, but act with transparent integrity. It involves willingness to be overruled, to jettison role-playing and status-seeking, to be ready to cast a single vote with everyone else. It involves

putting the welfare of the body of Christ before all personal advantage, success or reputation and it involves co-equal sacrifice for the Lord and his gospel. It is the leadership of those who are content to stand among the saints as those who serve.[59]

Pastors as Shepherds

Finally, let's return to Ephesians 4:11-12. Today there are some in the body of Christ who would deny the need for leadership in a local assembly of Christians. They are disturbed that many leaders act, not like servants, but like kings. They also point out that the earliest followers of Jesus were strangely silent about leadership and authority. In all of Paul's letters, for example, only once are leaders mentioned in the opening salutations, and then only in passing (Phil. 1:1).

But we must be careful not to throw the baby out with the bathwater. The New Testament presents a clear picture of how the early Christians viewed themselves. They understood each church to be an extended family (an institutionalized church was unimaginable) that practiced plural leadership. This eldership was non-hierarchical (each elder was equal in authority to all the other elders) and arose from within those churches the elders would lead. Because the Lord Jesus is the Head of the church (Col. 1:18), the elders led by example, not by "lording it over" the church (1 Pet. 5:2). The elders' authority lay solely in their ability to "persuade" with the truth of the Word of God (see the use of *peitho*, "persuade," in Heb. 13:17).

Jesus told the apostles, "You are all brothers" (Matt. 23:8). By this he meant that his followers comprised a brotherhood, a family in which there are no classes of people. The church has only one class of members: blood-bought, born-again believers. Jesus explicitly forbade honorific titles among his people, emphasizing instead the truth that "Whoever exalts himself will

---

[59] *Philippians*, 40.

be humbled, and whoever humbles himself will be exalted"
(Matt. 23:12). Thus the New Testament knows nothing of a
prestigious pastoral office as traditionally conceived, nor is there
any evidence to support the idea of one professional minister
leading a congregation. In Ephesians 4:11, Paul mentions
apostles, prophets, evangelists, pastors, and teachers, but one
would be hard-pressed to identify a New Testament "pastor" by
name. The New Testament calls Paul an "apostle," Agabus a
"prophet," Philip an "evangelist," Manean a "teacher," but it
never identifies anyone as a "pastor." Indeed, the word translated
"pastors" in Ephesians 4:11 is a metaphor rather than a literal
term denoting an ecclesiastical office. Note the following
occurrences of *poimen* (and its plural *poimenes*) in the New
Testament:

- Matt. 9:36: When he saw the crowds, he was moved with
  compassion for them, because they were weary and
  scattered, like sheep without a **shepherd**.
- Matt. 25:32: All the nations will be gathered in front of
  him, and he will separate them one from another, as a
  shepherd divides his sheep from the goats.
- Matt. 26:31: Then Jesus said to them, "All of you will be
  made to stumble because of me tonight. For it is written:
      'I will strike the **Shepherd**,
      And the sheep in the flock will be scattered.'
- Mark 6:34: When Jesus got out of the boat, he saw a
  large crowd and was moved with compassion for them,
  because they were like sheep without a **shepherd**. So he
  began to teach them many things.
- Mark 14:27: Then Jesus said to them, "All of you will be
  made to stumble because of me tonight. For it is written:
-     'I will strike the **Shepherd**,
      And the sheep will be scattered.'

- Luke 2:8: Now in the same country there were **shepherds** living out in the fields, watching over their flock during the night.
- Luke 2:15: When the angels had left them and had gone back to heaven, the **shepherds** said to each other, "Let's go to Bethlehem and see what has happened, which the Lord told us about."
- Luke 2:18: All those who heard it were amazed at the things told them by the **shepherds**.
- Luke 2:20: Then the **shepherds** returned to their flock, glorifying and praising God for everything they had heard and seen, as the angel had told them.
- John 10:2: The person who enters by the gate is the **shepherd** of the sheep.
- John 10:11: I am the good **shepherd**.
- John 10:11: The good **shepherd** gives his life for the sheep.
- John 10:12: When a hired hand, who isn't the **shepherd** and doesn't own the sheep, sees a wolf coming, he abandons the sheep and runs away. So the wolf drags the sheep away and scatters the flock.
- John 10:14: I am the good **shepherd**. I know my sheep, and am known by my own.
- John 10:16: I also have other sheep that are not from this pen. I lead them also. They will hear my voice, and there will be one flock with one **shepherd**.
- Eph. 4:11: He also gave some to be apostles, some prophets, some evangelists, and some **pastors** [i.e., **shepherds**!] and teachers....
- Heb. 13:20: Now may the God of peace who brought our Lord Jesus back to life from the dead, that great **Shepherd** of the sheep, through the blood of the eternal covenant....

- 1 Pet. 2:25: For you were like sheep going astray. But now you have returned to the **Shepherd** and Overseer of your souls.

In light of the consistent usage of *poimen* in the New Testament, it is ironic that the term most frequently used today to describe church leaders – "pastor" – is found only once in the entire New Testament to refer to followers of Christ, and then only in the plural. The word itself simply denotes a "shepherd." It's an appropriate image. In Jesus' day, shepherds were without status. Theirs was a lowly, humble occupation. Thus the metaphor is fitting, for our Lord said, "The greatest among you must become like the youngest, and the leader like a servant" (Luke 22:26).

In short, the present-day concept of "the" pastor is far removed from the mind of God. There is not a scrap of evidence from the early period that Christian leaders were ever organized into an official "pastorate" or that they were ever referred to as "pastors." It was only later that the church adopted an Old Testament-based religious system replete with an altar, a Christian sanctuary (church building), and a special priesthood. Contrariwise, the New Testament doctrine of leadership is based not on a clergy-laity dichotomy but on the complementary truths of the priesthood of all believers and the gifts of the Holy Spirit. Genuine Christian leadership is always based on truth and trust, not on power. In the New Testament we find *functional* distinctions between the leaders and the led but no *hierarchical* divisions. The New Testament church was "shepherded" by elders, men of wisdom and maturity who had earned the respect of others.

Summary: Who Rules the Church?

How, then, does Jesus build his church, and upon whose authority? At least seven things may be said by way of summary.

1. Christ alone is the Head of the church. He is the only Senior Pastor (Matt. 28:18; Col. 1:18; Eph. 4:5; 1 Pet. 5:2).

2. Christ's authority is manifested in the assembly through the gifts and ministry of the Holy Spirit. All Spirit-filled believers are priests and are directly responsible to the Head (Rom. 14:4; 1 Tim. 2:5). Moreover, all believers have gifts and can minister in and to the assembly according to their giftedness (Rom. 12:3-8; 1 Cor. 12-14; Eph. 4:7, 16). The New Testament knows nothing of a clergy-laity division. All the members comprise a fully functioning priesthood. Various believers can teach the church, and the congregation is permitted to question them or add their own insights under the direction of the Spirit (Acts 20:7; 1 Cor. 14:29-35).

3. In each assembly certain believers are not only gifted by the Holy Spirit but are gifts of Christ to the church (Eph. 4:11). Their specific ministry is to teach the Word of God and to equip their fellow saints for works of ministry (Eph. 4:12).

4. Leaders in the assembly are extensions of the church and not over it (Phil. 1:1). They are older and more spiritually mature brothers ("elders") who are sensitive to God's voice and who obey that voice. Their function is to "oversee" the assembly, and the assembly properly recognizes their experience and gifts (Acts 20:28; 1 Thess. 5:12-13). These elders arise from within the local church where their life and character are known (Acts 14:23; Tit. 1:5).

5. Elders are appointed by the Holy Spirit (Acts 20:28) based on their maturity, their gifts, and especially their character (1 Tim. 3:1-7; Tit. 1:5-9). Churches do not appoint elders; they recognize them. Men function as overseers because they *are* elders and because they are gifted as pastors.

6. The New Testament always speaks of oversight in terms of a plurality (Phil. 1:1; 1 Tim. 4:17; Heb. 10:17; James 5:14; 1 Pet. 5:1-2). It knows nothing of a church with "a" pastor. For example, the Ephesian church had a plurality of elders, not one "pastor" (Acts 20:17); hence the "angel" of Revelation 2:1 cannot possibly be used to support a one-man pastor system.

7. Often one elder will have more influence in the assembly because of his gifts and experience. But such an elder is not a "senior pastor" (head honcho); he is simply a "fellow elder" (1 Pet. 5:1). Jesus specifically taught his followers not to take upon themselves honorific titles that set them apart from the "brothers" (Matt 23:6-12; Mark 10:35-45).

These principles are not to be held only in theory. They should become our joyful practice as those in submission to the Head of the Body, the Lord Jesus Christ. In light of these principles, we would do well to ask ourselves some questions:

1. Why do so many of our assemblies divide their leadership into a hierarchy of "senior pastor," "associate pastor," etc. when the New Testament makes no such distinction?

2. Why do so many of our congregations look for potential leaders outside of their own ranks instead of raising and training their own men for leadership?

3. Why do so many of our congregations fail to give members of the church an adequate opportunity to exercise their gifts, including the gift of teaching?

4. If all believers are priests and gifted, why do so many of our congregations place the responsibility for edification in the hands of a few professional "clergy"?

The tendency is for Christian leaders to go along with the crowd and never take an unpopular stand. Pastors and other Christian leaders can easily fall into the trap of going with the flow and trying to maintain the "sacred" status quo. But the bottom line of discipling is *obedience to Christ*, and churches are God's perfect laboratory for working out that obedience in terms of our everyday decisions. When Peter and John stood up to the religious authorities of their day, they were willing to go "outside the camp." They knew what rejection was like, they knew what opposition was like, they even knew what jail was like, yet they kept on going back there for the sake of the Word of God. They refused to bow, in any way, shape, or form, to the secular-religious power of their day. The term "acquiescence" was simply not a part of their vocabulary.

We Christians have become our own worst enemies through compromise and tolerance. As long as we refuse to go outside the camp and bear the reproach of Christ, we will deserve nothing but stinging criticism. Now is the time to go forward, and going "forward" means going "outside" – outside the established religiosity of our day. Standing outside the camp with Christ will take constant vigilance and care. Church elders must lead the way by praying, teaching, serving – and by encouraging a spirit of radical obedience to the Word of God in their churches.

The Politics of Jesus: Disarming the Principalities and Powers

The evangelical subculture, which prizes conformity above all else, doesn't suffer rebels gladly, and it is especially intolerant of anyone with the temerity to challenge the shibboleths of the Religious Right.

Randall Balmer[60]

One is either a good German or a good Christian. It is impossible to be both at the same time.

Adolph Hitler[61]

The Seduction of Politics

In his book, *Tempting Faith: An Inside Story of Political Seduction*,[62] David Kuo, former deputy director of the White House Office of Faith-Based and Community Initiatives, reveals how the Republicans in the Bush administration sought the votes of evangelicals but had no real interest in leading a new Great Awakening. "This [is the] message that has been sent out

---

[60] *Thy Kingdom Come: How the Religious Right Distorts the Faith and Threatens America* (New York: Basic Books, 2006), 168.

[61] Cited in Donald Durnbaugh, *The Believers' Church: The History and Character of Radical Protestantism* (Scottsdale, PA: Herald, 1985), 179.

[62] New York: Free Press, 2007.

to Christians for a long time now: that Jesus came primarily for a political agenda, and recently primarily a right-wing political agenda – as if this culture war is a war for God. And it's not a war for God, it's a war for politics. And that's a huge difference," said Kuo in an interview on 60 Minutes.[63] His point? Mixing evangelical faith and Washington politics-as-usual is antithetical to the Gospel.

Herein lies one of the greatest challenges of modern American evangelicalism. Today God and conservatism have practically merged into one. The "wonder-working power" of politics now drives a large segment of the Christian right.[64] But sin is our trouble, not liberalism in government. To treat cancer by temporary measures is to endanger the victim still worse. Whenever government tries to make men good without being righteous – something the devil would love more than anything in this fallen world – the professing church becomes cluttered with hosts of superficial saints who never sell out to Christ.

Anyone who reads the New Testament will see that Jesus refused to identify himself with any of the politico-religious parties of his day, whether they were called Pharisees, Herodians, Sadducees, or Zealots. Likewise, Christians today must maintain an ultimate commitment to Christ and eschew loyalty to a political party – *any* political party. It is indeed a decadent citizenry that rejects sound doctrine and heaps to itself politicians to tickle its itching ears. Yet who will deny that this is

---

[63] http://www.crooksandliars.com/2006/10/15/david-kuo-on-60-minutes-the-name-of-god-is-being-destroyed-in-the-name-of-politics/.
[64] The reference here is to George W. Bush's famous 2003 State of the Union speech in which he said, "The need is great. Yet there's power, wonder-working power, in the goodness and idealism and faith of the American people." As many have subsequently pointed out, the hymn "There's Power in the Blood" is not about the American people, or any people. It's about the wonder-working power of the "blood of the Lamb." Such statements by the president caused many of his critics to wonder if he hadn't confused genuine faith with national ideology. See http://www.whitehouse.gov/news/releases/2003/01/20030128-19.html.

happening? Mr. Kuo's experience is a reminder of how easy it is for well-meaning Christians to substitute political activism for genuine compassion. As long as good men try to remedy conditions with temporary palliatives there will be a need for prophets like David Kuo. That's because lostness – not liberalism, not libertarianism, not "compassionate conservatism" – is our problem. We are sinners, blind, even lepers, and to try to make people religious without making them righteous only makes them harder to reach with what they need most.

An American Theocracy?

During my foreign travels this past year I had the opportunity to read *American Theocracy* and *The Fall of the House of Bush*,[65] manifestos of the non-interventionist foreign policy wing of American politics. It was nightmarish reading at best. How is it, the authors asked, that the religious right has come to be defined by delusional idealism and religious zeal? How is it that so many American evangelicals not only approved but actually glamorized the Iraq War as a form of Christian "mission"? Had it not been for the alliance forged between the neoconservatives and the right we may well have avoided the greatest foreign policy disaster in American history. And now, marching to the same tune, the right is falling in step with the neocons in demonizing the Iranians. That America, rather than Saddam, is known today universally for torture and abuse and the killing of thousands of innocents should be decried by every evangelical Christian who believes in truth and justice. "Freedom is not America's gift to the world," said former President Bush in a 2004 address, invoking the Godhead. "Freedom is God Almighty's gift to each man and woman in the world."[66] But to confuse national pride with redemption and the cross is blasphemic. It is obvious that

---

[65] Kevin Phillips, *American Theocracy* (New York: Viking, 2006); Craig Unger, *The Fall of the House of Bush* (New York: Scribner, 2007).
[66] http://www.washingtonpost.com/wp-dyn/articles/A57466-2004Sep2.html.

unless there is a change of policy in Washington, a war with Iran is sure to occur sooner or later. It takes no great imagination to foresee this. "Unless we fight them over there we will have to fight them over here" is the unchallenged and unchallengeable mantra of the day. Some U.S. politicians – Congressman Ron Paul notably – have given good reasons why America should never start a war unless it is already necessary for self-defense. I think this is sound political advice, not to mention the fact that this is the historical American position. It is easy to understand why Americans might object to it. They have been taught, and have accepted, a Manichean view of the world: America is good, Islamic states are evil. I strongly disagree with this prevalent viewpoint. It is more than an embarrassment for the evangelical church in America that we have gone forth into the world with gun and Bible, flag and cross.

A Post-Political Church

Over the span of 33 years of teaching my understanding of the Christian faith and politics has changed in several significant ways. One of the most important is that I have come to identify myself not so much with the Reformers of the sixteenth century but rather with the Anabaptist dissenters whom they opposed (often to the death) – those simple men and women who believed that the church needed, not reforming, but rebuilding from the ground up. This process of rebuilding involved more than merely insisting upon believers' (or adult) baptism as the only legitimate form of baptism. Of far greater significance was the fact that the Anabaptists of the sixteenth century, precisely *because* they held to believers' baptism, taught that it was necessary for the church to be completely separate from the state, since the state included all members of society.[67] Moreover, because in their theology the church consisted only of believers, the Anabaptists were convinced that every Christian was a

---

[67] Today, of course, the principle of religious freedom has been written into the federal Constitution of the United States.

Gospel missionary and therefore must preach and evangelize in order to bring people to faith. Indeed, since Christ had commanded his followers to love even their enemies, it was impossible for a Christian to restrict love and service only to fellow Christians.

As we saw in chapter 3, the most unique aspect of the Anabaptist tradition was the belief that to be a Christian implied giving up everything in radical obedience to Christ. This emphasis has great relevance today. If modern believers accept the responsibility thus laid upon them by their Lord, they must continually be asking the question: What does radical discipleship mean for a modern Christian? How can we obey in every situation Jesus' command to love God and our fellow human beings, *including our enemies?*

Here again we are confronted with foundational concepts of discipleship. The claim of the Christian Gospel is that God, because of his unfailing mercy and love, offers to humanity forgiveness and reconciliation in the person of Jesus Christ. The church, therefore, is the community in which God's transforming love is known and translated into the world on his behalf. In this sense one could argue that early Anabaptism was the first modern missionary movement, prior even to the one launched by William Carey – which may help to explain why the Anabaptist movement spread like wildfire in its earliest years. As heirs to the Anabaptist tradition, Baptists likewise believe in missions and world evangelism. But while this may be our belief, our practices are frequently inconsistent with it. Many churches have forgotten that it is only through self-sacrificing love that God works to bring people into his kingdom. All of this, I think, is more-or-less self evident, but we have not taken it very seriously in fleshing out our ecclesiology. I think it is time we thought through our theory on this question anew, not to bring it into conformity with our practice, but to bring it in line with the Scriptures.

It is precisely this responsibility to witness and minister in the world that is avoided in our staid, bourgeois memberships, with their comfortable adjustment to laissez-faire capitalism and their unwillingness to question the political status quo. I wish we could sense how closely interwoven our religion and politics have become. For many evangelical Christians, religion has become the principal justification for political involvement. Thus everything that carries a "Christian" message is legitimized and justified in terms of political commitment. This is the new ecclesiology. No matter how biblically uninformed or banal the thought, any religious stance is legitimized thanks to the political message behind it. Has anyone failed to notice just how deeply "God-and-Country" nationalism has come to permeate American society? This is nothing but pure idolatry. I can understand our mass media allowing itself to be commandeered for propagandistic purposes. But as an evangelical who values highly the authority and inspiration of Scripture and the sole lordship of Jesus Christ, it is disturbing to see the church co-opted by the state for the same purposes.

"Christian" Politics?

Years ago Jacque Ellul warned us that the greatest danger to liberty in Western society proceeds from the military-political state born of a dream of utopian perfection on earth.[68] It seems clear to me that Ellul has touched on something of very great importance. As one who rejected out of hand the para-Marxist realism of my practical theology professors in Basel, I find it just as easy to part company with those on the theological right who argue that evangelicals should inject Christianity into politics. A close reading of the Gospels would show that the opposite is true. Neither Jesus nor his disciples ever engaged in or showed any interest in politics. Our Lord refused to be the political liberator of Israel. I fully agree with the Anabaptists that the state is meant to be secular and that a dualism exists between church and state, between political power and the proclamation

---

[68] Jacque Ellul, *The Presence of the Kingdom* (Philadelphia: Westminster, 1992).

of the Gospel. There is in my opinion neither "Christian" liberalism nor "Christian" conservatism. Equally valid (or invalid) perspectives can be found on both sides, but there are no *Christian* grounds for preferring one side over the other. If Jesus was a capitalist (or a socialist, or a Republican, or a Democrat, or a Libertarian), I fail to see anywhere in the Gospels where he has made that known to us. The fact is that political loyalties are always relative and determined for purely individual and conscience reasons.

To state that the church should reject any form of allegiance with politics does not, of course, imply the separation of church from society or that Christians should not hold or express political views. Quite the opposite is true. Acknowledging Jesus as Lord over all things means that we will seek to be biblically informed about our political decisions and discussions. But it does *not* mean that a Christian politician can claim to support distinctively "Christian" policies any more than an auto mechanic can claim that he practices distinctively "Christian" car repair. It is the duty of the church to penetrate society as salt and light – this is acknowledged by all – but it fails in that duty when it rubberstamps the platform of politicians of any stripe.[69] According to the Scriptures, the church is not a political community at all. It is a brotherhood that proclaims Jesus Christ as Lord and that expects the coming of his kingdom – or, to put it another way, a brotherhood that lives with a view to the time when Christ will ultimately prevail over all earthly kingdoms. The church knows, therefore, that it lives in the midst of an eschaton that has not yet come, and that the polar realities of the church and the world are the twin sociological units within which it lives. We must be very careful, then, not to confuse the kingdom of heaven with the kingdom of man even as we love and serve the world in Jesus' name. Whatever political differences exist

---

[69] This is one reason I do not support inviting a sitting president or cabinet member to speak at annual religious conventions.

between Christians can be transcended by the common ground of the cross and empty tomb.

As I have traveled around the world I have come to the reluctant conclusion that there is something fundamentally wrong with U.S. foreign policy and that the time has passed for glibly praising "the American way of life" without pondering the fact that our nation is as bitterly divided today as it was 140 years ago. Abu Ghraib is only one among many confidence-shaking events. Our government suffers from crippled leadership, and it is not just a few radical left-wingers who are saying so. Far too many of our national leaders have become power-intoxicated, self-righteous do-gooders, sure that their purposes justify their wrongdoings. The debacle of the Iraq War, the unprecedented budget deficit, the saber-rattling vis-à-vis other Middle-Eastern nations, all show how vulnerable our constitutional system is and reveal a deep-seated fear that the very moral fiber of our nation has been sapped of strength. No attempt to resolve the great policy issues of the nation can succeed unless we first of all face and solve the fundamental cause of our disillusionment: Government simply cannot fix society. The important thing is that the church live in the world as a community that demonstrates the Jesus quality of life. From a biblical point of view, questions of political affiliation or structure are strictly secondary.

The Just War Tradition and Pacifism

In short, our responsibility as Christians is not to do battle for the soul of the nation through political means. Yet insofar as the church is to sit in judgment on the world and its structures, believers in Jesus cannot avoid confronting issues of war and peace. Although I do not belong to a peace church or have a grand theory of nonviolence, I share the peace church ethos and am attracted more to the Radical Reformation than to Niebuhrian arguments. Put differently, I had been well enough educated at Basel to recognize what an extraordinary argument

Jacque Ellul and other theologians like him are making when it comes to church-state relations. I would not pretend to be a pacifist in any formal sense of the word, but then again I do not claim to be a theologian of any stripe. It is not my task here to present a biblical case either for or against pacifism. To develop a full-orbed theology of pacifism would require a lifetime of exacting scholarship.

Part of the problem is definitional. John H. Yoder identifies at least eighteen types of pacifism in *Nevertheless: The Varieties and Shortcomings of Religious Pacifism.*[70] In *Two Paths Toward Peace,*[71] James W. Child and Donald Scherer identify a variety of forms of pacifism, including (1) nonresistance, (2) the prohibition of all violence, (3) the prohibition of lethal violence, and (4) the rejection of organized violence between nation-states. Glen H. Stassen, in his essay "Just Peacemaking," offers an alternative view:

> We need another paradigm for ethics in addition to pacifism and the just war theory. When pacifism and the just war theory dominate the debate about war, the question narrows to whether it is okay to make war or not. What falls out of the debate is whether or not we should take peacemaking initiatives to prevent war. Jesus did not focus on when it is okay to make war but on peacemaking initiatives that he commanded us to take. We need a third paradigm, a just peacemaking theory.[72]

Yet I wonder. The words of Vernard Eller haunt me: "How, then, is it of any help to anyone for pacifists belligerently to demand that a secular society, on its own, in a secular world, proceed to pacify itself in a way the gospel suggests is possible

---

[70] Scottsdale, PA: Herald, 1971.

[71] Philadelphia: Temple University Press, 1992.

[72] Glen H. Stassen, "Just Peacemaking," *Christians and Politics Beyond the Culture Wars*, ed. David P. Gushee (Grand Rapids: Baker, 2000), 225.

only to a God of resurrection capability?"[73] Perhaps the best I can hope to do is to try and become active in the political arena with my Christianly-derived values, acting simply as a private citizen who is concerned about peacemaking rather than as an academic who espouses a supposedly infallible "theology" of pacifism. At best I am a simple Greek professor who is struck by how relevant Marpeck and Yoder, Grebel and Kreider, are to my life.[74] Their views on pacifism are only a small part of the contribution they have made to my own spiritual journey from an admirer of megachurch consumer religion to a proponent of nonconformist Christianity.

None of this is to say that I feel a special calling to defend pacifist views. Rather, I hunger and thirst for a tradition that understands what Christian discipleship really entails and that indeed does more than understand it but embodies it as well. Above all, I wish to preach what I practice and not assume that spending months abroad each year helping needy people in Africa or elsewhere means that I am able to tell others what the practice of peacemaking truly means. One thing I do know. If Jesus tells me to love my enemies and to pray for those who persecute Christians, it means that my love must be all-inclusive. Jesus' Sermon on the Mount is not about arbitrary ideals to be promulgated in a textbook but is a call to concrete action. I believe deeply that the disciple who truly wants to follow the Jesus paradigm will gladly follow his teachings about peacemaking.

Pacifism, if I understand it correctly, is not merely a rejection of modern warfare. It demands that we say "Yes" to the cross.

---

[73] Vernard Eller, *Christian Anarchy* (Eugene, OR: Wipf and Stock, 1999), 182.

[74] Just as John H. Yoder was a Mennonite who preferred to call himself an ecumenical neo-Anabaptist, so I am a Baptist who feels himself an heir to the Anabaptist heritage. I do not claim to be a thinker on the level of a John H. Yoder; I mention him simply to note that we share a passion to see the Anabaptist tradition rediscovered. (Coincidentally, we also have in common our Basel doctorates.)

This, of course, is the weakness of the just war tradition, [75] for it never calls on the Christian to accept the cross *in contrast to* waging war. Our witness to the cross must, then, be grounded primarily on the Gospel of peace rather than on a refutation of the just war tradition. The Constantinian church must give way to the Johannine church, the church militant to the community of the Crucified. As Oscar Cullmann has shown in his exegetical study *The State in the New Testament*,[76] the early church was an overcoming community centered on the cross. Christ himself was uninterested in the state and was certainly no "freedom-fighter." His response to the question about tribute (Mark 12:17) revealed his indifference toward the state and in the particular form of government under which he lived. In Matthew 5:39 he clearly condemns violent resistance. The apostle Paul likewise teaches that Christians are never to avenge themselves, in contrast to the state and its "sword" (Rom. 13:1-7). Does this imply, then, approval of the violent retaliatory code by the state? Hardly. James Douglass puts it succinctly:

> It must be recalled that Paul is writing in a tradition which had always affirmed God's, and now affirmed Christ's, lordship over all of history so that even sin, without being justified, was channeled into the movement of the divine through history. In this context wars are the judgment of God, a chastisement upon us for our infidelity to his word, but without thereby justifying the sin of those who bear down upon us with the sword. Thus the

---

[75] Along with Reinhard Hütter ("Be Honest in Just War Thinking! Lutherans, the Just War Tradition, and Selective Conscientious Objection," in *The Wisdom of the Cross*, eds. Stanley Hauerwas, Chris K. Huebner, Harry J. Huebner, Mark Thiessen Nation [Grand Rapids: Eerdmans, 1999], 69), I prefer the term "tradition" over "doctrine" because the just war tradition, although it has a fairly stable set of criteria, develops other criteria in which accommodations to new circumstances are constantly being made.

[76] London: SCM Press, 1957.

> prophet Isaiah had identified Israel's enemy, Assyria,
> as the instrument by which God chose to punish the
> Israelites for their sins – yet without justifying the
> Assyrians for their sins in so doing.[77]

We cannot forget Paul's teaching about Christ's complete and personal triumph over the "principalities and powers" at the cross (Eph. 3:10). This theme is reiterated in the Apocalypse, which proclaims Christ's victory over the powers (including the state) as the Lamb who was slain (Rev. 13:8). Thus the testimony of the New Testament to a nonviolent imperative is irrefutable. Christianity transcends national loyalties and state absolutes. However, just as the state was allowed to execute the Son of God, and just as the beast was allowed to "make war on the saints and to conquer them" (Rev. 13:7), so the church in suffering love must be prepared to endure persecution if need be. The church's historical capitulation to "Constantine's compromise" and its deepening involvement in violence and persecution do not invalidate the New Testament's strong witness to submission and nonviolence.

Given the all-embracing ideal of the New Testament, it is not hard to see why modern evangelical thinkers are beginning to reassess their position on pacifism and to return to the early Reformation principle of *sine vi, sed verbo* ("without force, but through the Word"). For many New Testament scholars, the only commitment that makes Christological sense for the church today in her response to the state is her commitment to a catholicism of the cross and the nonviolent ethic of pacifism, that is, an ethics revealed by Christ in the Gospel, an ethics of love "that does no harm to a neighbor." As Matthew 10:18 show us, the tension between church and state, between Jesus and his band of followers, will always be a reality. Even when the state makes a pretense at absolute authority, the believer is still to be subject. But this is a far cry from saying that the New Testament

---

[77] James W. Douglass, *The Non-Violent Cross* (Toronto: Macmillan, 1966), 195.

sanctions the state's conduct or that the Christian should take up the sword in its defense. Nonviolence is required because Christ requires it. Again, to quote James Douglass:

> Every disarmament agreement and every reduction of international tensions requires of its participants an act of faith in man which is just such a step toward the cross; the Christian will always ask one more step. He will never expect the governing authorities to embrace the cross, just as Paul did not expect them to, and he will remain subject to them in all that is just. But to render unto Caesar the things that are Caesar's is to bear in mind always that it was Caesar's cross on which the Lord of glory died, so that the Christian, too, may finally have to render to Caesar a cross rather than a denarius.[78]

Cross-Based Politics

If there is to be today a new politics of faith based on the cross of Christ, it will have to meet critically the issues raised by Augustine and Niebuhr. This means for me personally that it is not enough to question the just war tradition or to condemn the Constantinian compromise in the abstract. Nor is it enough to rail against the Christ-washed militarism being offered in his name by our politicians. Nor can I merely exegete Jesus' mandate in the Sermon on the Mount disinterestedly. The only responsible Christian ethic is for me to become an active participant in service and sacrifice for the sake of the Prince of Peace. I must discover what it means to rid myself completely of the baggage of self-will and to plunge into the tranquil sea of God's will where alone I will find joy. There are countless situations in my life in which I must decide to put the interests of others above my own life-interests. The power of nonviolence is an important step on the downward path of

---

[78] *The Non-Violent Cross*, 212-213.

Jesus, but only if I deliberately *chose* such a path can "peace on earth" begin to be realized. At the very least, this means for me:

- rejecting the mindset of Western imperialism
- refusing to support the notion that Christian missions benefits from the spread of empire
- preaching the cross instead of the protection of the sword
- placing love of enemy at the heart of the Gospel rather than at its periphery
- affirming an allegiance to Christ that transcends national boundaries or roles
- bearing witness of sacrificial service in the name of Christ
- helping to move peace toward the center of the church's witness in the world
- teaching about the alternative model provided by the historic peace churches
- living a life of radical discipleship
- engaging in polite dialog with just war theorists and Christian advocates of war
- sharing the biblical basis of peacemaking to persons genuinely seeking to know more about it
- being committed to a ministry of reconciliation
- being willing to suffer in the spirit of the cross and to undergo a literal baptism unto death if need be
- focusing on the cross as the center of my faith and life
- manifesting the firstfruits of the kingdom of peace in mutual aid and love with the community of faith
- repudiating any coercion or manipulation of faith by the state
- praying constantly that God would move to ameliorate the hatred and pride that provide the occasion for war

- struggling to perfect my life by the Holy Spirit in the confidence that the Lord is at work
- being nonconformist yet involved in attempts at reconciliation worldwide
- preaching the Gospel persuasively and powerfully in deed as well as in word
- maintaining warm Christian fellowship with all who sincerely follow the guidance of conscience with regard to military service, including those who feel obliged to render such service

In the end, while I cannot say that I am currently a peace church pacifist, this is irrelevant since pacifism, unlike the just war tradition, is not as much a dogma to be believed as a lifestyle to be practiced. One does not have to be a pacifist in the full sense of the word to be profoundly shocked at the violence in Iraq. The work of a genuine peacemaker must be to call civil governments to account and to help limit the violence when conflict is actually in progress. At the very least there is never any reason to glorify revolution or war or to utter blatantly warmongering statements such as were made by candidate John McCain in the run-up to the 2008 presidential election.[79] The Jesus paradigm requires both peacefulness and peacemaking, and

---

[79] In July 2008, McCain reacted to a report of rising U.S. cigarette exports to Iran by saying it may be "a way of killing 'em." See http://uk.reuters.com/article/email/idUKN0832180920080709. At a campaign meeting in South Carolina in 2007, McCain was asked if there was a plan to attack Iran. He began his answer with a variation on the lyrics of a well-known pop song, Barbara Ann. "You know that old Beach Boys song, Bomb Iran?" Then he sang, "Bomb bomb bomb, bomb bomb Iran" before discussing what he considered to be Iran's threat to international peace. See http://www.salon.com/opinion/conason/2008/03/21/mccain_iran/. Earlier, Jerry Falwell made headlines when he stated, "You've got to kill the terrorists before the killing stops. And I'm for the president to chase them all over the world. If it takes ten years, blow them away in the name of the Lord." Cited in Gregory Boyd, *The Myth of a Christian Nation* (Grand Rapids: Zondervan, 2005), 67.

the history of the church shows our urgent need to be reminded of these twin emphases again and again in view of the church's compliance with violence. The Anabaptist tradition, as we have seen, summons us to reclaim this peaceable teaching and example of Jesus.

For a variety of reasons – not least being faithfulness to the Lord who opposes coercive evangelism – the peaceable Christian will question the moral compromises and cultural capitulation of mainstream evangelical Christianity vis-à-vis the Middle East. Whatever one may think about the legitimacy of the current war in Iraq, terrorism cannot be fought without an understanding of its underlying causes (and not merely its symptoms). As Zbigniew Brzezinski points out in his book *The Choice: Global Domination or Global Leadership*,[80] only a careful global strategy can weaken the complex political and cultural forces that give rise to terrorism. There can be no question that among the contributing factors in the development of terrorism in the Middle East is America's tunnel vision approach to the world, that is, seeing the world in terms of "us against them." Whether or not the perceptions are true, the Muslim world views our "war on terror" as a Neo-Crusade against the world of Islam. Unless the sources of the motivations for terrorism are acknowledged and dealt with, attempts to eliminate terrorism will see little or no success. What creates terrorists has to be confronted and politically undercut.

Recently our war on terror has morphed into a campaign to vanquish all potential enemies (real or perceived) of United States hegemony – from Somalia to Iran to Syria. But American unilateralism has only produced rising anti-American political and religious hostility. After all, if the definition of a "rogue state" is one that causes inter-state disputes, the "Axis of Evil" nations are not the only states to deserve that moniker. When Ron Paul attempted to point this out during the Republican presidential debates in 2007 he was ridiculed for being anti-

---

[80] New York: Basic Books, 2004.

American and treated like a political leper by the mainstream media. His "crime" consisted of recognizing that certain motives and passions are driving terrorism worldwide. But he is right. To talk only about terrorists is to risk focusing solely on the symptoms of terrorism while ignoring altogether the more complex and deeply-rooted motivations behind terrorist attacks. As John H. Yoder has reminded us,[81] the just war tradition automatically implies the legitimacy of conscientious objection to war. In other words, wars may be just or they may be unjust. Ron Paul may or may not believe in the just war tradition, but it is not wrong for him (or anyone else) to suggest that a state can be waging an unjust war or to put the burden of proof on those who advocate the need for warfare in a particular case, since such reasoning is a logical implication of the just war tradition.[82]

---

[81] *When War Is Unjust: Being Honest in Just-War Thinking*, 2nd ed. (Maryknoll, NY: Orbis, 1996), 70-79.

[82] In his brilliant essay "The Reception of the Just War Tradition by the Magisterial Reformers," *History of European Ideas* 9 (1988), 20-21, John H. Yoder concludes:

> Before the Reformation, the just war tradition was an inchoate body of distinctions and rules of thumb whereby confessors, canon lawyers and moralists hoped to restrain war, once it was clear (since the Constantinian establishment) that they could not forbid it. The intent to restrain evil was sincere. It could issue in penitential disciplines. For the early Martin Luther it could (hypothetically) demand selective conscientious objection.

> *After* the Reformation, the ordinary meaning of the mention of the "just war" in the creeds, to the ordinary Protestant, clerical or lay, was the opposite. War is all right. Those who reject it are condemned by name. The sovereign who sends his subjects to war is *prima facie* trustworthy as a judge of cause and means. The way is open for citizen-soldiers and for uncritical Protestant patriotism. There should be no surprise that the first strong modern objection to total war in the light of the just war tradition should have come from Roman Catholics.

Conclusion

That the religious right has become bellicose, belligerent, and militaristic is difficult to deny. The tragedy is that prominent evangelicals are at least partly responsible for helping to shape America's utopian foreign policy and worldview. But perhaps the greatest irony of all is that those who were so sorely misled as to the reasons for the invasion and occupation of Iraq are the same people who are eager to accept the same flawed arguments for invading Iran. War based on false pretenses is never justified. On the other hand, a negotiated settlement to our differences with Teheran may contain some unexpected blessings. General William Odom, President Reagan's director of the National Security Agency, in an article entitled "Exit From Iraq Should Be Through Iran," has written: "Increasingly bogged down in the sands of Iraq, the US thrashes about looking for an honorable exit. Restoring cooperation between Washington and Tehran is the single most important step that could be taken to rescue the US from its predicament in Iraq."[83] Yet General Odom's recommendations have yet to be taken seriously in Washington.

If evangelical ethicists believe that a just war case can be made for invading Iran, let them make it. I for one will listen carefully and prayerfully to what they have to say. Thus far I remain unconvinced. After all, as Dr. Lindy Scott has shown in an essay published by the Center for Applied Christian Ethics at Wheaton College, the just war tradition let us down miserably when we went to war with Iraq.[84] Another Christian ethicist, David Gushee, has also raised concerns about America's response to 9/11. "Six years after 9/11, our nation is less secure, less powerful, less free, less respected, less democratic, less

---

[83] http://yaleglobal.yale.edu/display.article?id=9223.

[84] Available at http://www.wheaton.edu/CACE/. Some, indeed, on the right have attempted to argue that the invasion of Iraq was justified. Perhaps the most determined to do so is Jean Bethke Elshtain, *Just War against Terror: The Burden of American Power in a Violent World* (New York: Basic Books, 2003).

constitutional, and less fiscally sound than we were on that bright, clear, terrible morning," he writes. Gushee concludes with these words:

> In general, the American churches have lacked the political independence, the discernment, and the courage even to understand and name what has gone wrong, let alone to resist it. A domesticated church has been employable as a servant of the state, even to the point of defending torture.

> It seems to me that 9/11 in a way unhinged our nation and sent us hurtling down the wrong path. But the American church bears considerable responsibility for its inability to stand fast on the solid rock of Jesus Christ in the midst of this unhinging – yet one more reason to bow our heads in sorrow on 9/11.[85]

It is my conviction that an unjustified attack on Iran will only take America further down the path of self-destruction and will make it even more difficult to penetrate the Muslim world with the life-changing Gospel of Jesus Christ. As Dietrich Bonhoeffer has noted:

> The command, "you shall not kill," and the Word "love your enemy," are given to us simply to obey. Every form of war service, unless it be Good Samaritan service, and every preparation for war, is forbidden for the Christian. Faith that sees freedom from the law as a mere arbitrary disposal of the law is only human faith in defiance of God. Simple obedience knows nothing of the fine distinction between good and evil. It lives in the discipleship of

---

[85] http://www.apbnews.com/2739.article.

Christ and does good work as something self-evident.[86]

I realize that many of my readers, even those who share my theological convictions, will find some of my opinions in this chapter to be different from their own. Crucial and controversial issues will continue to be debated until our Lord returns. The purpose of this chapter is to suggest that Christians on both ends of the political spectrum can be unified under the reign of Christ in service to his Gospel. This does not mean that we cannot disagree about the threat of terror, nuclear proliferation, foreign policy, environmental quality, and justice for the poor. At the same time, all evangelical Christians should be united in a common commitment to peacemaking and to living out the countercultural lifestyle of Jesus' kingdom without being beholden to the politics of either the right or the left.

---

[86] Dietrich Bonhoeffer, *No Rusty Swords*, ed. Edwin H. Robertson (London: Collins, 1970), 166.

The Future of Christianity: Habits of the Upside-Down Kingdom

The biggest problem facing Christian theology is not transition but enactment .... No clever theological moves can be substituted for the necessity of the church being a community of people who embody our language about God, whose talk about God is used without apology because our life together does not mock our words.

Stanley Hauerwas and William Willimon[87]

Upside-Down Deviants

It's time to summarize and conclude. Are you in a mainstream congregation? In an emergent church? In a home meeting? It really doesn't matter. The paramount question to ask is this: Are you willing to wash the feet of others? Are you willing to use your gifts to enrich the Body of Christ? Are you willing to forego pyramids of power? Are you willing to surrender what is rightfully "yours"? In the end, it doesn't matter what evangelical church we belong to. What matters is that we faithfully pursue the Jesus paradigm regardless of the religious structures around

---

[87] *Resident Aliens: Life in the Christian Colony* (Nashville: Abingdon, 1989), 170-71.

us. What matters is that we work from the bottom up. "Don't be arrogant," writes Paul, "but be friendly toward humble people" (Rom. 12:16). "Go out of your way to show respect for one another" (Rom. 12:10). And we are to do this whether or not we agree with our brother or sister in every area.

One of the most important aspects of walking with Jesus is learning this lesson of serving different parts of the Body in times of special need, even if that means sailing against the prevailing winds. While growing up in Hawaii I well remember facing the local draft board during the height of the Vietnam War. I knew I would be applying for a status that would be frowned upon by certain members of my local church, many of whom were serving in the U.S. military at one of the many bases on Oahu. I also had a very practical dilemma. I had grown up in a single-parent family. I had no car. My mother had no car. How was I going to get from Kailua to the draft board office in Kaneohe? So it was with great trepidation that I approached my pastor to ask him for a ride. He was from the heartland of America and a vocal supporter of the war. He knew my position, and I knew his. But when the day of my appointment came, my pastor was happy to drive me to the draft board office. He sat patiently outside for over an hour as I argued my case. When I emerged from the meeting with a smile on my face he congratulated me cheerfully even though he held to a different position. He was willing to respect my decision, and our unity around Christ that day gave corporate witness to the love of Jesus. Today when I look back on that experience 42 years ago I think of how Paul described unhypocritical love in Romans 12:9-16 (selected verses): "Love sincerely. Be devoted to each other like a loving family. Go out of your way to show respect for each other. Be energetic as you serve the Lord. Share what you have with God's people in need. Be happy with those who are happy. As much as is humanly possible, live in peace with everyone." It can only have been divine love that motivated my pastor to do what he did for me that day. God's love supersedes all self-interest.

When Jesus told us to love our neighbor, he meant it. Moreover, such love is indiscriminate, as Jesus' parable of the Good Samaritan teaches. *Everyone* is my neighbor, even my "enemy." When Jesus violated the religious laws of his day in order to serve human needs, he modeled this kind of love. Paul's letter to the Romans makes it clear that we are to take the initiative in extending unconditional love to others. "Don't owe anyone anything except to love one another," Paul writes, "for the one who loves another has fulfilled the law" (Rom. 13:8). I like how Donald Kraybill puts it: "The disciples of Jesus are upside-down deviants. They exceed conventional expectations. They take the initiative. They don't discriminate between enemies and neighbors."[88]

As an example of such "deviant" love, let me take you with me to Ethiopia. I had been teaching at a college in Addis Ababa when I got news that a 19 year-old Christian had been murdered for his faith in a village south of the capital. So along with one of my Ethiopian colleagues I drove there to visit and pray with the parents of the deceased. I knew there was little I could do for that grieving family except to wrap my arms around them. It was a Saturday afternoon when my companion and I, accompanied by some of the local church elders, drove out to the family's village along a long, dusty road. There we enjoyed sweet fellowship – not the superficial social fellowship that we are so used to in our churches here in America, but the kind of oneness, common love, and concern that Paul describes so wonderfully in Philippians 2:1-4. As dusk approached we began to drive back to town. All of a sudden I noticed some lights off in the distance. I asked the men who were with me, "What are those lights?" "That's the prison," they replied. "Is Yisak[89] there?" I said. "Yes," came the answer. (Yisak was the young man who had murdered the 19 year-old Christian. He had been tried and sent to prison.) When I heard that Yisak was there the

---

[88] *The Upside-Down Kingdom* (Scottsdale, PA: Herald, 2003), 180.
[89] Not his real name.

Lord immediately said to me, "Go and visit Yisak in prison."
You ask, "Was the voice audible?" No, it was deeper than that. I
simply had a very strong impression that I needed to visit not
only the victim's family but also the murderer himself. When I
asked the elders if it was possible for me to call on Yisak, they
stared at me as though I were out of my mind. "You want to
visit the murderer?" they replied with open-mouthed
astonishment. "Yes, if that's possible," I said.

Despite their misgivings, the elders were able to arrange a
meeting between me and Yisak for the next morning. When we
arrived at the prison we were ushered into a meeting hall where I
was asked to wait until Yisak could be led to us from his cell.
Slowly the hall began to fill with prisoners, all of whom were
curious about this white-faced foreigner. When the hall was full,
the warden turned to me and asked me if I would like to speak
to the group. Of course I agreed, and for 15 minutes I shared
with them the story of Jesus and how he loves them and how he
can forgive *any* sin. When I had finished speaking, the prisoners
began filing out of the hall. One prisoner, though, stayed
behind. He remained seated, head in hands, weeping
uncontrollably. It was Yisak. Somehow he had been led into the
room and I had not noticed it. I went up to him, introduced
myself and the elders who were with me, shared a few words
with him, gave him a blanket that I had purchased in town, and
left. God had clearly done a miracle in arranging for Yisak to
hear the Gospel that day.

One of the main reasons I wrote this book was to give a
heart's cry for a great awakening in the area of missions. So
often as Christians we seem to be more concerned with minor,
ephemeral matters than with the real basics of the Gospel. In
my career as a seminary teacher I have to admit I was not always
in the kingdom-building business. I confess it's been a struggle
for me to find the balance between my professional life as an
academic and my life as a simple follower of Jesus. In our
current techno-urban society, there is so much pressure to
conform to "churchianity," a form of Christianity that considers

"relevance" more important than service and sacrifice. For me personally, this involved an overcommitment to the academy and an undercommitment to Christian community and discipleship. Gradually I began to see the need to take seriously Jesus' announcement that he had come to preach the Gospel to the poor. He had status, but he didn't exploit it. He had power, but he used it to serve the needs of the outcast and stigmatized. He was willing to serve others even at the risk of his own life. I began to see that those who are greatest in the kingdom are those who not only teach but also do the commandments of God (Matt. 5:19). I began to understand that nationality, education, and social status mean nothing to Jesus. I started to see that in his kingdom there are no small people. Above all, I began to repent of my hankering after prestige and comfort.

A few months after I first visited Yisak I went back to see him again. In fact, I visited him whenever I was in Ethiopia (about every 6 months). One day Yisak asked me for a Bible, which I gladly supplied. About two years after our first meeting, my wife and I were visiting Yisak when he said to us, "I'm ready." We asked him, "What are you ready for, Yisak?" He said, "I'm ready to acknowledge Jesus as my Lord and Savior." And in the middle of the prison he lifted his hands toward heaven and cried out in Amharic, "Yesus Getano!" ("Jesus is Lord!"). At that very moment the kingdom of God invaded that Ethiopian prison, the kingdom of forgiveness, peace, and joy. Like the apostle Paul, Yisak was a murderer, but now he was forgiven. Suddenly Yisak became very quiet. He looked at us in the eyes and said, "My family told me that if I ever became a follower of Jesus they would disown me. They would not visit me when I got sick or bury me when I died." Then he said, "*You* are now my parents." At that very moment Yisak became our responsibility, along with eight other Ethiopian youth whom my wife and I care for. We would tell people, "We have nine Ethiopian children, and one of them is in prison for murder."

Do you see how Jesus' love is indiscriminate? Do you see how it obliterates the category of friend and enemy since everyone is our neighbor? I'm happy to say that the elders began visiting Yisak regularly in prison. They too have forgiven him – and have been forgiven of their spite.[90]

Doing the Kingdom Together

Since I have begun my walk along the downward path of Jesus, I have visited several foreign countries where Christianity is illegal. I have shared the love of Jesus with many people, including high government officials. Today, almost all of my vacation time is spent traveling from country to country in Eastern Europe or Central Asia or Africa. One of the things I've learned during my travels is that God's love is more powerful than human hatred. Jesus went boldly to the Samaritans and engaged them in conversation because he loved them. He overturned social customs and religious expectations. He violated turf rules by going into "enemy" territory. For some reason, God has allowed me to do the same thing today. Wherever I go I think of what Martin Luther King, Jr., said just before he died: "To our most bitter opponents we say: Throw us in jail and we will still love you. Bomb our houses and threaten our children and we will still love you. Beat us and leave us half dead and we will still love you. But be ye assured that we will wear you down by our capacity to suffer. One day we shall so appeal to your heart and conscience that we shall win you in the process, and our victory will be a double victory."[91]

Recently my wife and I began working in an area of Ethiopia where there are very few Jesus followers. We work closely with the local evangelical congregations that have banded together for the sake of the Gospel. Token unity isn't enough for them. In the endless race of status escalation, their pastors have set aside

---

[90] While in prison Yisak led several people to the Lord. Last year he was released – 8 years early – on good behavior. He is now preparing to become a traveling evangelist.

[91] "The American Dream," speech, Ebenezer Baptist Church, Atlanta, GA, July 4, 1965.

personal ambition to engage in inconspicuous service so that
their neighbors might be evangelized. Such cooperation is so
important to me that I wrote about it at my website.

> [W]e have intentionally adopted a cooperative model
> of missions. We will gladly work with any Christ-
> centered evangelical church that is willing to answer
> Christ's call to obedience and self-sacrificing love.
> We don't have to see eye-to-eye on secondary issues
> to work hand-in-hand. John Newton, author of
> "Amazing Grace," once wrote to a fellow pastor:
> "What will it profit a man if he gains his cause, and
> silences his adversaries, if at the same time he loses
> that humble, tender flame of the Spirit in which the
> Lord delights, and to which the promise of his
> presence is made?" We believe that the whole Body
> of Christ can and must submit itself to its Head, the
> great Redeemer of mankind. This is the very heart
> of Christianity – disciples of Jesus following Him in
> obedience and love. In Him we are all one family in
> which each member is given a grace gift, a
> functional service to carry out for the good of all.
> We are all brothers in Christ, members of one
> spiritual family, parts of one spiritual Body.[92]

I'm well aware that doctrine is vitally important. We can't
pretend to have unity where there isn't any. I am fully committed
to the task of training people to think biblically and to engage in
serious Bible study while at the same time presenting them with
the truth of a world vision. I have no argument with people who
are concerned about doctrinal purity. I share their concern. But
when we take secondary and even tertiary issues of belief and
make them the main issue, then we have set aside the vision we
read about in Acts 1:8 and Matthew 28:19-20. Jesus calls his
disciples – all of us – to be equally committed to his cause and

---

[92] http://daveblackonline.com/how_we_do_missions.htm.

equally concerned to take his love to the ends of the earth. There is no substitute for loving our neighbors as we love ourselves, even when they don't think and look like us.

It is time we did the kingdom – together. Inter-denominational cooperation demands flexibility in our ideals, though it should never threaten essential Christian doctrine. But doctrine is not the same thing as personal conviction. In the midst of the complex debates going on in the church today, my position is that we need a balanced approach. Above all, we need to be sure we are working together to build God's kingdom and not our own. We need to face up to the reality that a high proportion of mission work will never be accomplished unless we can work past our denominational loyalties. In northern Ethiopia my wife and I gladly work with Baptists, Pentecostals, Lutherans, and Mennonites, to name but four evangelical denominations. Nobody is trained in missiology. Nobody is a professional evangelism strategist. But all of us agree that God can achieve tremendous things through the most unlikely people. Thus far we have sent out ten evangelists two by two into five different villages, where they share the Good News passionately and cheerfully. Twice a year I teach them for a week, using only the Bible as my textbook. In southern Ethiopia, where the evangelical church has existed for much longer, our work is more diversified. God has used us to construct meeting halls, support evangelists, provide reading glasses for the elderly, give out protein bars and pre-natal vitamins by the thousands, distribute over 6,000 Amharic Bibles to children (who had to earn them by memorizing Scripture passages), and open a health clinic. My wife and I are not with any mission board or NGO. Instead, we prefer to be completely self-supporting in our work so that every penny that comes to us goes to where the needs are the greatest. However, although we are independent missionaries, we are not mavericks. We work closely both with the leaders of the churches in Ethiopia and with the leaders of the churches here in the States that have an Acts 13 vision.[93]

The Gospel of Hospitality

In short, ever since I realized that down is up, I have become an activist in the cause of missions. Notice that I said "the cause of missions" and not the cause of homeschooling (although my wife and I home educated our children), or elder-led congregationalism (although I espouse it), or the weekly observance of the Lord's Supper as a full meal (although I believe this is what the New Testament teaches). Fundamentally, my wife and I want to be known as "Great Commission Christians," people burdened by the needs all around us, including the "ends of the earth." For this reason we frequently open our home to retreatants from all over North America and even foreign countries to stay with us for free. We know that God can use quietude to bring healing and focus to our lives. Romans 12:13 says "share what you have with God's people in need" and "pursue hospitality." Paul's language implies a habit or pattern of life, not an occasional activity. It also emphasizes the effort and cost of showing hospitality – we are to "pursue" it. The idea is that costly hospitality is something to be practiced at all times, not just during holidays or when it is convenient. Our homes should exist not just to meet our own needs; they should be constantly ready for hospitality – an eagerness to welcome people who don't ordinarily live there. Peter says we are to "be hospitable to one another without complaining" (1 Pet. 4:9). Perhaps we could call this the Gospel of Hospitality – "Gospel" in that it is based on the cross of Christ. This Gospel of Hospitality invites people to come with their hopes and failures and questions to a place where they will be unconditionally accepted. It is a place of refuge for the weary traveler. It welcomes the stranger, the neighbor, the pilgrim. Our only

---

[93] For more on the Lord's work in Ethiopia, see our "Ethiopia Files" at Dave Black Online: http://daveblackonline.com/ethiopia_files.htm.

motivation is the fact that, being ourselves recipients of God's hospitality that made us members of his household, we now have the joy of becoming conduits of his hospitality to others.

It is natural for us, in our busy schedules, to neglect hospitality. That's why Hebrews 13:1-2 says, "Don't forget to show hospitality to people you don't know. By doing this some of you have shown hospitality to angels without even being aware of it." God is pleased when we open our homes and hearts to others in this way. My wife and I have pursued several hospitality strategies, including:

- inviting our neighbors to our home
- sharing food with others
- paying attention to people when they visit (i.e., stopping what we are doing and shutting off such distractions as the radio)
- asking about a person's food preferences and allergies when a meal is involved
- greeting people warmly
- entertaining students in our home
- regularly visiting shut-ins and the sick
- opening our farm to individuals and families for retreats
- providing privacy as best we can
- involving guests in regular family activities if they desire to participate

Like Francis and Edith Schaeffer, founders of L'Abri in Switzerland, we have discovered that the simple act of receiving guests is an increasingly important part of our life together. We even designed the physical architecture of our new home to enable hospitality. Our concept of "retreat" has no programs or scheduled activities. We simply desire to provide an atmosphere that will simulate spiritual growth. We delight in welcoming people into our home, and I have no doubt that we have "shown hospitality to angels without being aware of it."

There are far too many inhospitable homes in our communities. Call for a return to biblical hospitality and people will resent it because it may require a change of priorities. Elders and deacons are required to show hospitality, but there is no double standard with God. What is good for elders and deacons is good for all of Jesus' disciples. In a day when stopping for hitchhikers is risky and befriending foreigners almost unheard of, God says, "Don't forget to show hospitality to believers you don't know." And these "strangers" are often closer than we think – children with special needs, abused women, grieving widows or widowers, foreign workers, international students, pregnant teenagers, elderly neighbors. Jesus doesn't expect us to do everything. But even if we can't end homelessness we *can* take in one stranger. Even if we can't heal the sick we *can* visit them. Even if we can't empty the prisons we *can* visit a prisoner. Hospitality is not easy. It goes against the grain of our contemporary values. It involves hard work, planning, and efficiency. And it can be inconvenient. But it will not occur in our lives until we make it a deliberate priority.

For my wife and me, *spiritual* priorities have become paramount in our life as a married couple. I think we are discovering what Paul meant when he wrote to the Corinthians, "Because the time has been shortened, those who are married should live as though they are not" (1 Cor. 7:29). We too are feeling the same sense of urgency. In the same letter, Paul says that an apostle has authority to take with him "a sister, a wife" (1 Cor. 9:4). Note the order: first sister, then wife. There is great wisdom here. My wife and I are deeply in love with each other. We are crazier about each other today than we have been in 33 years of marriage. But just as importantly, and even more importantly from an eternal perspective, we are brother and sister, fellow workers, and fellow soldiers for Christ. Just before his execution, John Perry wrote a letter to his wife from the Tower of London and signed it: "Your husband for a season and your eternal brother, John." The happiest married couples I know are those who are dedicated to something bigger than themselves. This is the work of the Holy Spirit. It cannot be taught in marriage enrichment seminars. It is learned in the crucible of life.

To put it another way, Christian marriage is about Jesus and his kingdom. It is not about self-fulfillment. It will involve more than a cursory relationship with one's spouse. Can you pray and serve together for the needs of others? Do you help each other discover and develop your gifts? We have developed a "no-nonsense" approach to our marriage. We count the effectiveness of everything we do in terms of the expansion of the kingdom. We are learning *how* to spend our time. We have set aside time for ministry – whether it's entertaining guests at Bradford Hall or taking two or three mission trips abroad each year. Our prayer is, "Lord, make us saltier so that we might make others thirstier!" We work together as a team, hopefully under the direction of the Holy Spirit. Because we both love Jesus, we seek to do what pleases him. We have gladly made significant changes in our lifestyle and rescheduled our time so that more of our energy and resources can be put into working for funding and encouraging the work of the kingdom. Have we always lived this way? Hardly. But we are gradually tasting the joy of sacrificial giving, and we are looking forward to learning even more of what that means in the years ahead.

How's Your Serve?

My reason for strongly emphasizing these points is one that will perhaps offend some people. It is this: urgency demands that we place a greater value on people than on our supersized sanctuaries or our well-paid staffs. We can no longer depersonalize the poor in the world to the point where we feel comfortable spending more on ourselves than on others. In particular, I have joined my voice with the voices of others in exposing the dangers of nationalism and political idolatry. Don't be tricked, Jesus said, into thinking that my kingdom is of this world. Don't believe the lie that the way up is up. Don't forget that those who are despised, forlorn, and weak are the ultimate recipients of God's blessing. We cannot "barter" with kingdom ideas. Jesus welcomes only nobodies into his kingdom. "This, in a nutshell," writes Gregory Boyd, "is the primary thing God is up to in our world."

> He's not primarily about getting people to pray a magical "sinner's prayer" or to confess certain magical truths as a means of escaping hell. He's not about gathering together a group who happen to believe all the right things. Rather, he's about gathering together a group of people who embody the kingdom – who individually and corporately manifest the reality of the reign of God on the earth. And he's about growing this new kingdom through his body to take over the world.[94]

If you talk like this or – better yet – *live* like this, you are liable to lose a significant portion of your congregation. Many of God's people have drunk so long from that old depressing cocktail of politics that they will not tolerate a call to sobriety. There may even be disappointment and heartbreak before people realize how deeply they have played the power game. Seeking the kingdom doesn't mean an easy lifestyle or a smooth path. The important issue for us to face is this: How can we continue to give God the scraps off our tables when he requires everything?

Simply stated, we must practice serving. It's the most underused power in the world. It doesn't matter where we live or work. Our community will be richer and far better off if we decide to get involved. Simply read your local newspaper and you'll discover all sorts of opportunities to influence others for Jesus. You might visit the local nursing home or homeless

---

[94] *Myth*, p. 30.

shelter. Or you might help with administration, work in a thrift store, cut grass, stuff envelopes, or call on the sick and homebound. The opportunities are endless to model the Jesus paradigm to others. Your involvement will be an incredible example to others around you who are looking for a role model. Don't wait for politicians to bring about cultural renewal. Be the hands and feet of Jesus – evangelizing the lost, feeding the hungry, teaching the illiterate, caring for unwed mothers, rebuilding the broken walls of our culture. "The central lesson of the last one hundred years is that the state can disrupt, but it cannot save families," concludes Allan Carlson.[95] If we want to build a caring society, good deeds speak louder than words. Societal renewal is not ultimately a political task but a spiritual mission. We need to take ownership of the towel and basin Jesus offers us. We must be willing, as Jesus was, to bend over and serve the helpless irrespective of status or social custom. Jesus not only taught but modeled the downward path. He embodied it by being an advocate for the outcasts. He said that we are to love others as he loved us. Isn't that plain enough?

That is why it is dangerous for you to read this book. The more we know about the kingdom, the greater our obligation to live for it. We are not called to be Americans. We are not called to be Baptists. We are not called to be Republicans or Democrats. We are called to be foot-washers. If you feel like you are a failure in this regard, join the club. But don't despair. Jesus is quick to notice every simple effort to please him. And we please him most when we make sacrificial service in his name the core, not the caboose, of our lives.

---

[95] *Family Questions: Reflections on the American Social Crisis* (New Brunswick, NJ: Transaction Publishers, 1991), 279.

Afterwords:

A New Paradigm for Theological Education?

As I have said in this book, in the last few years God has been rewiring my priority system. You see, rather than seeking status or privilege my goal now is to make as many disciples of Jesus before I go to heaven as possible. Notice I said disciples and not simply converts. When I was in college, I "went witnessing" every Saturday during my freshman year. I guess I was pretty good at it too. However, the Holy Spirit began to show me that Jesus wanted lifelong followers who were committed to obedient followership, not mere hangers-on who from time to time hit the piñata of heaven for goodies. I still shared my faith, but not "on the run" any more. I began going down to Watts (South-Central LA) on a regular basis and just hanging with the dudes there, playing pickup basketball and trying to presence God's love among these tough and hurting kids. Can God use cold-turkey evangelism? Yes. But today I much prefer relationship building, even though it takes more time and effort.

My goal, then, is to serve the Lord Jesus by sharing his love with others both relationally and relentlessly. This does not mean, however, that I am not involved in writing and scholarship any more. Indeed, I am doing more writing than ever. But my idea of theological education has also changed in the past few years. In this book I have argued that the seminary exists to serve the world, not only the church. Instead of being oriented primarily toward pastoral care of congregations, theological education must refocus on training men and women to be the people of God humbly serving the nations. I recall reading the story of the founding of one of America's largest and best known evangelical seminaries. The founder's purpose in starting the school was to establish a training center for evangelicals who would preach the Gospel in every corner of North America. Through the years, however, the seminary moved further and further toward a knowledge-based paradigm and toward becoming a school for professional ministry. This also happened to many other evangelical institutions of higher education. Most seminaries today are knowledge-based and classroom-dependent. The professional paradigm drives their curriculum. Ministry has become detached from God's mission in the world.

In his book *Thank God, It's Monday!* William Diehl remarks:[96]

> In my opinion, our seminaries are ... so victimized by their own academic institutionalism that not only are they failing to prepare the clergy for the role of equipping, but they are also supporting a philosophy which depreciates a theology of the laity.... Thus, the theologians inadvertently define what a church institution really is – an inward focusing principality which sustains its own life by directing all wisdom and training to those who have committed their lives in professional service to it.

All of this would have been completely foreign to the earliest Christians. In their outstanding book *God's Frozen People*,[97] Mark Gibbs and Ralph Morton describe the learning environment of the first- and second-generation church:

---

[96] William Diehl, *Thank God, It's Monday!* (Philadelphia: Fortress, 1982), 190-91.
[97] Mark Gibbs and T. Ralph Morton, *God's Frozen People* (London: Fontana, 1964), 20.

There was plenty of theological study and discussion. Indeed it could be argued that in no subsequent age was there so much theological education. But it was carried out in the whole of the body of the church. It was not a specialist study for the training of the professional servants of the church. Paul's letters were not written to be studied by ordinands in theological colleges; they were written to be read in church and to be studied by all the members of the church.... It was an unruly and chaotic training in theology but it was open to all and all could contribute.... It was carried on in the midst of the noisy life of the church and was shared by others, merchants, slaves and women, all of whom made their contribution. It was a theological education for the people of the church – it was lay, not clerical.

This is one reason I want to see biblical education returned to the local church as much as possible. In-ministry formation is, I believe, the best means of producing servants who can lead the church. The focus would not be on profession or licensure or ordination or degrees but on shaping leader-catalysts who are committed to mobilizing a whole army of evangelicals to be on mission in the world in the power of the Holy Spirit. Leaders would see their role as mobilizing the people of God for sacrificial ministry to the nations, including their own. The local congregation would again become the locus of training, wherein natural leaders are recognized by the church for their giftedness. These leaders, in turn, would guide the church into the doctrine of the priesthood of all believers not only in regard to ministry and mission but equally in regard to the interpretation of Scripture. Whatever programs are developed would be seen not as preparation for ministry but as opportunities to enhance the ministry that is already taking place. The goal would no longer be to enlarge church membership but to train people who are committed to God's mission in the world. Congregations would become not only the primary training center for ministry but the primary sending agency for their missionaries. To be a Jesus-follower would no longer mean "going to church." It would mean confessing and living out the Gospel of Jesus Christ as Lord of the *whole* of life. It would mean working together as the people of God with other denominations in proclaiming the Good News to all the peoples of the earth.

Undoubtedly, this would entail a radical paradigm shift in our thinking about theological education. Christian action in the world would become our primary focus. We would no longer major on the minors. The professional paradigm would be replaced by a renewed emphasis on in-ministry training of all believers. Congregations would begin recognizing leaders who were called and formed in their midst rather than simply hiring employees with degrees in divinity. Pastoral servant-leaders would become equippers of God's people for works of service. Most important of all, the evangelization of the world would no longer be considered optional but recognized as the reason the church and the seminary exist.

God's basic call is a call to mission. Our main purpose as the church is a redemptive one. We are called to pursue the Great Commission, to make disciples of the nations, to build Christ's kingdom worldwide. What happens on Sunday morning is only the beginning of what it means to be Christ's Body.

It is by God's unmerited favor, and by the atoning death of Christ on our behalf, that we are saved, delivered from divine judgment, and made partakers of a heavenly calling. But God did not pay such a price merely to shine us up a bit. It is sadly possible to enjoy saving grace in uncompromising orthodoxy without much serving grace in obeying the Lord Jesus. The church needs to learn how to walk as he walked who took the form of a lowly servant in order to "seek and to save that which was lost." One sure mark of genuine revival is that it sets the people of God to sharing the Good News. What showers of blessing can fall if we would only obey our Lord's command to go into the entire world and preach the Gospel to every creature.

For many years now missions has been my heartbeat – more than my scholarship, more than my books, more than my personal comfort. Saving grace is serving grace. Our Lord Jesus came to set the world on fire. We need to rekindle the evangelistic flame of God in our marriages, our homes, our churches, and our denominations. Let us confess and cooperate with God by throwing out the stuff that is displeasing to him and recommitting ourselves to a Gospel- and kingdom-driven lifestyle.

Topical Index

145

Scripture Index

150

Person Index

Disciples:
Jesus With Us

by Riley Richardson

with Henry Neufeld

Looking for *More*?

Here is a place to find 'it'!

Suggested Retail: $7.99

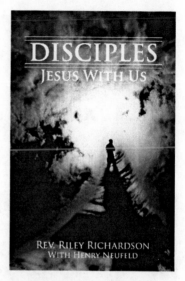

"**The key to church renewal is very simple: *every follower of Jesus is to live what is believed.*"** – David Alan Black, *The Jesus Paradigm*, **p. 27**

This book was written by a pastor concerned with discipling those people who came to the Lord in his church. Riley Richardson has a passion for evangelism, yet he found few resources to use with new believers.

This book is basic. Don't buy it to study the theology of discipleship. The chapter titles tell the story:

1. *What Have I Done?*

2. *Prayer*

3. *Joining with Others*

4. *Bible Study*

5. *Service*

6. *Gifts*

7. *Moving Onward*

Help the new believers in your congregation live what they now believe.

Who's Afraid of the

Old Testament God?

by *Alden Thompson*

A *FRESH* look at the Old Testament!

$9.99

Are you hesitant to study the Old Testament? Afraid of what you'll find? Do the laws and customs seem strange and irrelevant to you?

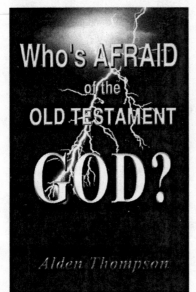

Take a journey with Dr. Alden Thompson as he finds the grace of God in the Old Testament stories and even in some of those strange laws.

As Alden often tells classes: "You may not like the Old Testament, but Jesus did!"

Here are the chapter titles:

1. *Don't let your New Testament get in the way of your Old Testament*

2. *Behold it was very good and then it all turned sour*

3. *Whatever happened to Satan in the Old Testament?*

4. *Strange people need strange laws*

5. *Could you invite a Canaanite home to lunch?*

6. *The worst story in the Old Testament – Judges 19-21*

7. *The best story in the Old Testament – the Messiah*

8. *What kind of prayers would you publish if you were God?*

From the Participatory Study Series:

The Gospel According to St. Luke: A Participatory Study Guide

The Gospel of Saint Luke: A Participatory
Study Guide is the newest installment to the
successful Participatory Study Guide Series
from Energion Publications. This series
emphasizes individual and community
involvement in the Bible story, inviting
students to become part of God's activity in
the world by acting on and sharing what they
learn.

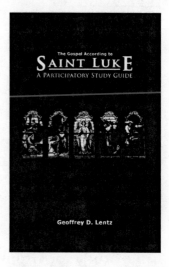

Written by Geoffrey D. Lentz, associate
pastor at First United Methodist Church,
Pensacola, FL, this study guide gives the
seeker historical insight and a fresh look into
the Jesus Christ that Luke sought and
recorded. Geoffrey brings his love of
Church history and great thought-provoking
questions into a user friendly layout that
promotes lively discussions and deep-rooted
growth in a group study.

Each lesson includes suggestions for prayer, exercises, thought questions, and
basic background information on the passages studied. References to study
Bibles and other useful resources are provided.

Also available: **To the Hebrews: A Participatory Study Guide** and
Revelation: A Participatory Study Guide

Coming in the fall of 2009 ...

Learning and Living Scripture: A Guide to the Participatory Study Method

Henry Neufeld and Geoffrey Lentz, a teacher and a pastor, will team up to
present this method of study in a practical, usable way. Learn to integrate
prayer and scripture reading while also being faithful to the historical meaning
of the text and its use throughout history by the community of faith.

This guide is not just about study and learning facts; it's about letting the God
who gave scripture live in and through you as you learn and share.

To order, visit any major online retailer, or see our web site at:

EnergionDirect.com
http://www.energiondirect.com

Phone: (850) 525-3916
P. O. Box 841
Gonzalez, FL 32560

More from Energion Publications

Personal Study

When People Speak for God	$17.99
Holy Smoke, Unholy Fire	$14.99
Not Ashamed of the Gospel	$12.99
Evidence for the Bible	$16.99
Christianity and Secularism	$16.99
What's In A Version?	$12.99
The Messiah and His Kingdom to Come:	
A Biblical Road Map	$19.99 (B&W)
	$49.99 (Color)

Christian Living

52 Weeks of Ordinary People – Extraordinary God	$7.99
Daily Devotions of Ordinary People – Extraordinary God	$19.99
Directed Paths	$7.99
Grief: Finding the Candle of Light	$8.99
I Want to Pray	$7.99

Bible Study for Groups

To the Hebrews: A Participatory Study Guide	$9.99
Revelation: A Participatory Study Guide	$9.99
The Gospel According to St. Luke:	
A Participatory Study Guide	$8.99
Identifying Your Gifts and Service:	
Small Group Edition	$12.99
Consider Christianity, Volume I & II	
Study Guides	$7.99 each

Politics

Preserving Democracy (Hardcover)	$29.99

Generous Quantity Discounts Available

Dealer Inquiries Welcome

Energion Publications
P.O. Box 841
Gonzalez, FL 32560
Website: http://energionpubs.com
Email: pubs@energion.com
Phone: (850) 525-3916